# KATHRYN KELLY

## THE MOLL BEHIND "MACHINE GUN" KELLY

### BY
### BARBARA CASEY

Published in the United States of America by:
Strategic Media Books, Inc.
782 Wofford St., Rock Hill, SC 29730.
www.strategicmediabooks.com

Manufactured in the United States of America.

ISBN-10:1939521491
ISBN-13:978-1-939521-49-1

Requests for permission should be directed to:
strategicmediabooks@gmail.com

or mailed to:

Permissions
Strategic Media Books, Inc.
782 Wofford St.
Rock Hill, SC 29730

Distributed to the trade by:

Cardinal Publishers Group
2402 North Shadeland Ave., Suite A
Indianapolis, IN 46219

*For Al,*

*With my love*

# TABLE OF CONTENTS

# PROLOGUE

*Several years ago, thousands of our citizens shivered in fear of a kidnapper whose name had much to do with the terror he engendered: he was called Machine Gun Kelly. However, there was someone far more dangerous than Machine Gun Kelly. That was Machine Gun Kelly's wife.*

J. Edgar Hoover, 1938, *Persons in Hiding*

In Oklahoma City, the case was being tried in the building that housed the post office, federal offices, and courthouse. Surrounded by armed officers, entry into the courtroom was allowed only with a pass after taking an elevator to the seventh floor and then climbing two flights of stairs to the ninth floor. In addition, everyone was required to be "patted down." Inside, there wasn't an empty seat available, the "electric air charged with excitement," as it was reported on film. It was the first time movie equipment with sound had been permitted in a federal courtroom.

There were other "firsts" as well. It was the first kidnapping trial after the passage of the "Lindbergh Law," making kidnapping a federal crime. It was the first major case solved by J. Edgar Hoover's evolving and powerful Federal Bureau of Investigation. It was the first crime in which defendants were transported by airplane. And, at the time, it was the largest ransom ever paid—two hundred thousand dollars, the equivalent of about three million dollars in today's currency. The date was October 12, 1933, and George "Machine Gun" Kelly and his wife, Kathryn, were on trial for the kidnapping of wealthy Oklahoma City oil man, Charles F. Urschel.

From the old photographs and film footage that have survived, George appears uneasy and sullen, wearing a dark suit, silk tie, and white shirt; and even though smoking was forbidden in the courtroom, cameramen captured him smoking several cigarettes. The facial cuts and large bump on the side of his head that he had received from federal agent J. C. White two days earlier are also visible.

Kathryn seems to have enjoyed the attention as she fluffs her hair and smiles confidently into the flashing and whirring cameras and posing for newsreel cameramen from Fox, Paramount, and other agencies that had followed them to Oklahoma City from Memphis where they were arrested. Fashionably dressed in high heels, a black satin dress decorated with feather epaulettes, and a hat perched jauntily on one side of her head, the members of the press and spectators alike were captivated by this tall, attractive, green-eyed brunette.

Many brought their lunch so as not to lose their seats. Some members of the press noted the "Roman holiday" atmosphere. Everyone watched as Kathryn and her husband, the notorious Machine Gun Kelly, awaited their much-anticipated verdicts.

# CHAPTER 1

## Cleo Lera Mae Brooks

Cleo Lera Mae Brooks was born in Saltillo, Mississippi, in 1904, the daughter of James Emory and Ora Brooks. Ora came from a long lineage of American ancestry. Born Ora Lillian Coleman to Thomas "Bud" and Mary Coleman in Mississippi in 1862, many of the Coleman clan moved to Coleman, Texas, living off and on in Oklahoma as well. Ora's great-grandmother, Martha Elizabeth Belue, was a full-blood Cherokee, born in South Carolina. She married Hezekiah Coleman who, according to family records, was also Cherokee. As a veteran from the War of 1812 he received land grants in Mississippi. Ora's education and that of her three sisters included music and social elocution. Ora married James Emory Brooks in 1903, and a year later they had one child, Cleo Lera Mae Brooks in Saltillo, the birthplace of Elvis Presley's mother.

Cleo Lera Mae was named after Cleo Epps, Tulsa's former one-room school marm-turned "queen of the bootleggers" who was found dead at the bottom of a septic tank, the victim of a revenge killing. Disliking the association and wanting to be called something more "glamorous," Lera changed her name to Kathryn when she dropped out of school at the end of her seventh grade, "bored by dull school work." By the age of fourteen, she was married to a laborer named Lonnie Frye, and they had one daughter named Pauline. That marriage quickly ended in divorce, and "Kathryn" and her daughter moved with her parents from Mississippi to Oklahoma, where she was briefly married again in El Reno, Oklahoma, to L.E. (Allie) Brewer. This marriage also ended in divorce.

It was about this time that Kathryn's mother, Ora, divorced James Emory Brooks and married Robert K.G. Shannon. Born November 12, 1877, in Naylor County, Arkansas, to Wilbur and Jemima Shannon, Robert, or "Boss" as he was known, was the sixth child of a hard-working farm family. Although some historians say that Robert received his nickname because of his political power in the Democratic Party, most agree that his mother gave him the name when he was a toddler. The Shannon family moved to Hood County, Texas, sometime prior to 1900. Four years later, Boss returned to Arkansas and in 1904 married Mary Icye Jackson, the daughter of a family friend. Eventually, they settled in Wise County where Mary Icye died at the age of twenty-five, leaving two young children. Boss returned to Arkansas and married Mary Icye's nineteen-year-old sister, Maude. They lived in Justice Precinct 4, Wise County, on property located about four miles outside of Paradise, Texas, where they had three more children. In 1923, Maude died and was buried near her sister, Mary Icye, in the Cottondale cemetery.

With the two older children taking care of the three younger ones, Boss worked his farm and raised cattle until the drought and the economy began to take its toll. In 1928, Boss married Ora Brooks in Parker County, Texas, and took Ora, Kathryn, and Kathryn's nine-year-old daughter, Pauline Elizabeth Fry, to his farm located near Paradise, Texas, north of Fort Worth where he got into the bootleg business.

It was the era of Prohibition. Formally known as the Volstead Act and called the "greatest social experiment of modern times" by President Calvin Coolidge, it provided for easy profits to be made by the illegal sale of alcoholic beverages (defined as anything more than one-half of one percent alcohol).

It was during this period that the country was just recovering from World War I—the "War to End All Wars"—and there was created the Agricultural Adjustment Act of 1933 designed to aid farmers in difficult times with federal subsidies and low-interest loans. The Great Depression was devastating the rich and poor alike; and many across the country were waking up to find themselves in the midst of the Dust Bowl. It was a time referred to by historians and journalists as the "Dirty Thirties."

Images from across the country included long breadlines, make-shift relief camps, protest marches and severe dust storms sweeping over the western plains. This reality, as stark as the images, was only made worse by the stock-market crash in 1929 and the national income fell by almost half. Out of desperation, many turned to activities that were illegal in order to survive. "Public enemies" such as John Dillinger, the Ma Barker gang, and Bonnie and Clyde, just starting to enter into the consciousness of America, were looked upon more as heroes rather than criminals as they traded gunfire with police and agents from a fledgling Federal Bureau of Investigation. It was in this environment that Ora, who worked in a grocery store, soon joined her husband in his bootlegging operations in order to make ends meet. For additional income, the couple also rented out rooms to criminals on the run for fifty dollars a night at their ranch near Paradise, Texas.

Wanting to leave the old, weather-beaten farmhouse for a better life, Kathryn left her daughter, Pauline, behind to be taken care of by Ora and Boss along with his five children and, at the age of twenty-nine, married a Texas bootlegger named Charlie Thorne. This was Kathryn's third marriage, and, like her mother, she soon got involved in the bootleg business, often making the illegal deliveries.

Not long after they were married, while away visiting relatives, she learned that Charlie was cheating on her. On the way home, she stopped to get gas and told the station attendant that she was on her way to Coleman, Texas, "to kill that God-damned Charlie Thorne." It wasn't the first time she had threatened to kill her husband. The next day Thorne was found shot to death with Kathryn's gun. Even though Thorne was illiterate, he had left a typed-written note that included his typed signature claiming that he "couldn't live with or without Kathryn. Hence, I am departing this life," the note stated.

At first the coroner ruled that Kathryn had shot Charlie in self-defense. Later, in spite of the rumors that Kathryn had threatened to kill Charlie on numerous occasions, and a general knowledge that Charlie, who couldn't read or write, had probably never used the word "hence" in his life, a coroner's jury ruled that Charlie had died of a self-inflicted gunshot wound between the eyes, thereby making it a suicide. The locals believed otherwise, however, claiming that the coroner and Kathryn were "friends."

Apparently criminal behavior ran in Kathryn's family. In addition to her mother's bootlegging operation, she had two uncles serving time in Leavenworth, one for stealing automobiles, the other for counterfeiting. Her aunt was a prostitute and her cousin was a bootlegger. Over the next few years Kathryn was arrested several times for various crimes, including robbery in Oklahoma City where she was convicted as Mrs. J.E. Burnell. This was later reversed on appeal. She also spent time in jail for prostitution and for receiving stolen goods. It is reported that in order to avoid arrest for a robbery she was involved in, she disposed of a packet of diamonds worth over ten thousand dollars by flushing them in a hotel toilet. In Fort Worth, Kathryn was convicted of shoplifting as "Dolores Whitney," but was released on a technicality without returning the money.

With that money and the money she had from her deceased husband, Charlie Thorne, she was able to improve her wardrobe and spend hours listening to jazz in the clubs and bars she patronized around Fort Worth. Working as a manicurist in Fort Worth at this time, Kathryn was frequently invited out on dates by local businessmen. Quite often, they would wind up on a deserted road where the businessman would be hijacked. Afterwards, by their prearranged agreement, the thief would split the money with Kathryn. One businessman in particular told a friend that the innocent little girl he was going to show a good time took him "to more speakeasies, more bootleg dives, and more holes in the wall than I thought existed in all of Texas. She knows more bums than the Police Department. She can drink liquor like water. And she's got some of the toughest women friends I ever laid eyes on!" It was a story that J. Edgar Hoover liked to repeat years later.

With her good looks, free spirit, and taste for the "better things" in life, Kathryn never lacked for male companionship. She became involved with another bootlegger, R.L. "Little Steve" Anderson, known as "Tulsa's leading bootlegger," who was doing business with a dark Irish southerner who called himself George R. Kelly. There is some speculation that Kathryn was responsible for "Little Steve" hiring George, and that she had first met George at Leavenworth while he was serving time on a conviction of bootlegging and she was at the prison visiting her uncles.

Other accounts have Kelly meeting her for the first time at a Fort Worth speakeasy where he was meeting with his new rum-running partner "Little Steve" Anderson. Kathryn was "Little Steve's" girlfriend. Whether it was at Leavenworth or through his association with "Little Steve" that Kathryn first met George, it wasn't long before they fell in love. Kelly used his undersized cache of bootleg and bank robbery money and oversized boasts of his business activities to dazzle Kathryn into accepting his proposal of marriage; and on September 30, 1930, after taking "Little Steve's" Cadillac and pedigreed bulldog, they drove to Minneapolis where they were married by a Methodist minister.

They seemed well suited for one another. Katherine took pride in her husband's criminal activities, and the material things they could afford as a result, including Chanel gowns, expensive furs, and diamond jewelry. In 1933, after the Kellys became famous criminals, a story published in *The Tulsa World* stated that Tulsa businessmen who bought illicit liquor from the affable Kelly joked with him about the risks he took by selling liquor from his briefcase. The "society bootlegger," he was called. The story also stated that Kelly's sleek black hair and pleasant personality endeared him to "Little Steve's" wife, Kathryn. There are no records that indicate Kathryn and "Little Steve" were ever married, although "Little Steve" told *The Tulsa World* that he married Kathryn and employed Barnes for five years, until his pedigreed bulldog disappeared. "I don't mind the dirty so-and-so [Kelly] taking my wife and my car," he said in the interview, "but I wish he'd left that dog." Kathryn was identified in subsequent news stories as Kelly's wife although there was no mention of a divorce from Anderson or of a wedding to Kelly.

# CHAPTER 2

## George Frances Barnes, Jr.

**A**ccording to the biography Bruce Barnes wrote of his father, Machine Gun Kelly was born George Frances Barnes, Jr., on July 18, 1900 in Chicago, Illinois. Other records indicate that George was born in Memphis, Tennessee, either in 1895 or 1897. He was the only son of George Francis and Elizabeth (Kelly) Barnes. Reared in a Catholic, upper-middle-class family, George's relationship with his father, an insurance company executive, was contentious from an early age. He had a sister, Inez, who was four years older, but it was his sickly mother George was especially close to.

When George was two years old, the Barnes family moved from Chicago to Memphis where they bought a two-story home at 2080 Linden, still standing today, on the corner of Rembert and Cowden in

Central Gardens. He attended Idelwild Elementary School and Central High School where former teachers, when interviewed years later, said he "didn't apply himself."

While still in high school, George was already involved in bootlegging using the family automobile, something he had angrily coerced his father into in return for not telling his mother of an on-going affair George, Sr. was having. During his sophomore year, George was arrested for possession of liquor. His father bailed him out, and by using his influence and status in the community, prevented George from serving time. But the hostility between father and son only deepened. Before George graduated from high school, his mother, Elizabeth Kelly Barnes, passed away. George was devastated and blamed his mother's death on his father's infidelity. It was a breach that was never mended.

After dropping out of high school his senior year, George enrolled as a probationary student at Mississippi A & M (today Mississippi State University) to study agriculture. During the first semester, he received thirty-one demerits; and twenty-four more during the first weeks of the second semester. In an attempt to get his demerits erased, he climbed the school flagpole and repaired a pulley. His highest grade was a C-plus, which he received in Physical Hygiene. He also received a zero in Woodwork and an incomplete in Military Science.

Realizing that the only reason he had enrolled in college to begin with was because his mother wanted him to, George left school on January 27, 1918, and returned home to Memphis where he quickly developed a romantic interest in a pretty young coed he met at a party.

Geneva Ramsey, also of Memphis, was from a well-to-do family and was a senior at Central High School at the time. Her father, George F. Ramsey, a successful businessman, knew of Barnes' reputation and forbade his oldest daughter to see him. In an effort to prevent a relationship from developing between his daughter and George, he had Geneva transferred to Columbia Institute at Columbia, Tennessee, to complete her final year of high school.

However, Barnes was persistent, and in 1919 the young couple eloped across the Mississippi state line. Geneva was eighteen years old; Barnes was nineteen. When their car broke down, they hitched a ride with two young men to Clarksdale where they were married. The following day Geneva contacted her girlfriend, Earlene Brewer, the daughter of the governor of Mississippi, who invited the newlyweds to stay with them. After partying for a few days, the newlyweds returned to the Ramsey family household.

George Ramsey proved to have a positive influence in the life of his new son-in-law, perhaps fostering the father/son relationship that Barnes never had with his own father. Years later while serving time in

Alcatraz, Barnes told his younger son, Bruce, "If your Granddad Ramsey had been my father, my life would have been entirely different." Ramsey, a successful levee contractor in the Mississippi River Valley, gave Barnes a job as commissary clerk with his company. Barnes' attempt at clean living, however, became derailed when George Ramsey was killed in an accidental dynamite explosion.

Ramsey's widow sold the business and tried to help her daughter and son-in-law get a fresh start. A used car business didn't work out, and neither did a goat farm located out on Poplar Pike. For a while George drove a cab with the 784 Taxi Company. Out of desperation, Barnes turned to his father for assistance. George, Sr., put his son in contact with another insurance agent who gave him a job. When this didn't produce the results the younger George wanted he turned back to bootlegging, the one thing in which he had achieved some success, and for a short time he operated a still near present-day Ridgeway. The still was discovered, however, and Barnes was sentenced to six months in the county workhouse.

Geneva didn't want any part of it. Once, after he was arrested and she had to borrow two hundred dollars from her mother to bail him out, she threatened to divorce him. By this time the couple had one son, George, Jr., whom they called Sonny. Barnes was starting to drink heavily and was not a good father or husband. During one heated argument with Geneva, Barnes picked up his young son and threw him across the room. Later, Sonny would fear and resent his father and never have anything to do with him.

The abuse continued, causing Geneva to leave Barnes on several occasions for short periods of time, only to return. She suffered one miscarriage before she had a second child they named Bruce. For whatever reason, Barnes doted on this child, often showing favoritism in front of Sonny.

With so much turmoil at home, Barnes left for Kansas City where he got a job in a grocery store as a checker. Once more he convinced Geneva to give him another chance, and she and the two young boys soon joined him there. With plenty of food on the table and special treats for her two sons, things seemed to get better for a while. When Geneva discovered a short time later that George was stealing from the store, however, she took her two sons back to Memphis, leaving Barnes for good.

It was an ugly separation where George tried to take her son, Bruce, and threatened to kill her family. At one point he asked Langford Poland Ramsey, Geneva's brother, to intercede on his behalf, but Lang didn't want to get involved in the domestic crisis. George was desperate and even attempted to return to the Catholic Church which he had neglected since his mother's death.

When that failed, in a fit of deep depression, he tried to kill himself by taking bichloride of mercury. The poison made him sick and caused extreme pain, and he ended up calling an ambulance for himself. At the hospital, George received no sympathy from his bitter father who coldly told him, "George, why don't you stop botching up every move you make in your life? The next time you try something like this, use a gun and make a clean job of killing yourself."

He didn't receive any sympathy from Geneva either, who was later granted a divorce, having to "advertise notice... because I didn't know where to reach him," she told reporters in 1933, when by then she was remarried as Mrs. F.X. Trimbach. "He was running in bad company."

Barnes, now completely on his own, began his final downward spiral as he turned to crime full-time. He remained in Kansas City for a while and developed a small bootlegging business. He also began using the name George R. Kelly, apparently to escape law enforcement officers, but also to preserve the good name of the family. "My family are good people. Only I turned out to be a heel," he would tell Alcatraz Warden James Johnston years later.

The middle initial "R" stood for Ramsey, the name of his deceased father-in-law. By taking on several partners, Barnes, now going by the name of George Kelly, expanded his bootlegging operation into Texas, Oklahoma, Tennessee, and Mississippi. Eventually, after purchasing additional trucks, he expanded into Santa Fe, New Mexico, where on March 14, 1927, he was tried and convicted for bootlegging, fined two hundred fifty dollars and sentenced to several months in the state penitentiary. He was arrested again on July 24 in Tulsa, Oklahoma, for vagrancy. His next arrest, however, was for selling liquor on an Indian reservation which constituted a federal crime. He was sentenced in federal court at Third and Boulder in Tulsa, and received as George Kelly, #29362, at the federal penitentiary in Leavenworth, Kansas, for a three-year term.

Author Myron Quimby describes George Kelly at that time as "a large man, with a round face and blue eyes, who was always grinning when he wasn't boasting. He was not exactly handsome, but women found him attractive, and he did have a natural air of good humor about him. His one big failing was his mouth. He could never keep it closed. He was a big blusterer who eventually came to believe his own lies." Federal agents would later describe him as having "extremely close-set ears, an unusually thick neck, and very dark complexion."

While in Leavenworth, Kelly was befriended by Texas bank robber Charlie Harmon, Frank "Jelly" Nash, who was serving a twenty-five-year sentence for a twenty thousand dollar train robbery at Okesa, Oklahoma, in 1923, and Francis Jimmy Keating and Thomas Holden, who were doing a similar stretch for a one hundred thirty-five thousand dollar train robbery at Evergreen Park, Illinois, in 1926. In late February, 1930, Keating and Holden walked out of the federal prison using faked passes. Kelly and Harmon, who worked in the photography department at

Leavenworth's records section, were accused by prison officials of helping with the forgeries. In fact, this was something Kathryn would confirm to FBI Agent in Charge W.A. Rorer later when trying to negotiate the release of her mother and herself from federal prison.

Keating and Holden headed for St. Paul, one of the cities along with Kansas City that was considered a safe haven for underworld figures because of their corrupt city government. After his own parole, Kelly joined the two men in the Twin Cities, probably at Harry Sawyer's Green Lantern Saloon at 545 ½ Wabasha in St. Paul. Sawyer was a local bootlegger who rented hideouts to the many criminals visiting St. Paul. He also delivered payoffs to police officials, assuring the gangsters immunity from arrest. Under the reign of his predecessor, Dan Hogan, there had been the added stipulation that the gangs could commit no crimes within the city limits. This part of the agreement, however, had fallen apart when Hogan was killed by a car bomb in 1928.

Frank Nash escaped from Leavenworth the same year that Kelly was paroled, and he, too, traveled to St. Paul. When Charlie Harmon was released in 1930, he joined Holden and Keating.

On July 15, 1930, Keating and Holden invited Kelly to participate in robbing the Bank of Willmar, located in a small town in Minnesota about one hundred miles west of St. Paul. Also at the robbery were Harvey "Old Harv" Bailey, Verne Miller and Sammy

Silverman. The gang stole an estimated seventy thousand dollars—worth about nine hundred thousand dollars today—and as much in securities.

But it was not a clean robbery. A cashier was pistol-whipped, and two women were injured when one of the gunmen shot off a round of bullets from his tommy gun. "I can't remember a holdup in the history of the state since the raids of the Younger Brothers and Jesse James gangs which compares to the one at Willmar for daring and cold-blooded disregard of human life," the head of Minnesota's Bureau of Criminal Activity claimed. The *St. Paul Pioneer Press* called it "one of the most daring bank holdups since the days of the Younger Brothers' and Jesse James' gangs."

The violence continued when a month later after taking an oversized share of the stolen money from the Willmar robbery, St. Paul homeboy Sammy Silverman and two associates from Kansas City were found shot to death at White Bear Lake in a wooded area fourteen miles northeast of St. Paul. During a prison interview in 1934, Kelly claimed that Miller had committed the murders after Silverman had "double-crossed him." At the time of Kelly's statement, Miller was already dead at the hands of the mob because of his participation in the Kansas City Massacre.

# CHAPTER 3

## Lovers and Partners in Crime

After getting married, George and Kathryn returned to Fort Worth and quietly set up house-keeping on Mulkey Street in the house that Kathryn's late husband, Charlie Thorne, built. Neighbors later recalled seeing the Kellys drive around in their big sixteen-cylinder Cadillac and how well dressed the couple were. George was to lament years later that this was the turning point in his career, and that he should have stayed in Tulsa bootlegging.

Also in September of that year, George helped rob a bank in Ottumwa, Iowa, with a group of bandits that included Holden, Keating, Bailey, Miller, Fred Barker and Larry DeVol, an associate of the Barkers and Alvin "Creepy" Karpis, given the nickname "Creepy" because of his sinister smile and called "Ray" by his gang members.

Concentrating in the "crime corridor," which stretched from Texas to Minnesota, and focused especially in the three states of Missouri, Oklahoma and Kansas, on April 8, 1931, Harvey Bailey, Frank Nash, Verne Miller and "Dutch Joe," who had participated in the Willmar Bank robbery a few months earlier, robbed the Central State Bank at Sherman, Texas, of forty thousand dollars. They escaped in a black Buick to Caddo Lake, near the Louisiana state line, where Kelly met them with a second getaway car—a Cadillac.

In September 1932, Kelly, Albert Bates, and Eddie Bentz, a seasoned bank robber, traveled to Colfax, Washington, near the eastern edge of the state, where, on September 21, they robbed the First Trust & Savings Bank of Colfax of seventy-seven thousand dollars. Within weeks, police raided the Kellys' home in Fort Worth, but the couple had already fled. Bentz was arrested a short time later in a Dallas post office. He admitted to knowing Kelly and Bates, and acknowledged they had a hideout on a ranch somewhere in Texas, but denied any involvement in the Colfax robbery. When Bentz was able to make bail, he fled the state.

A short time later, Kelly struck a bank nearby at Denton. Then on November 30, 1932, he along with Bates and Chicago hoodlum Eddie Doll, robbed the Citizen's State Bank near Kathryn's birthplace at

Tupelo, Mississippi, stealing close to forty thousand dollars. After the robbery the bank's chief teller would say of Kelly: "He was the kind of guy that, if you looked at him, you would never have thought he was a bank robber." All total, Kelly was involved in six bank robberies between March 1930 and November 1932.

Bruce Barnes writes that his father felt superior to the bank robbers he befriended in Leavenworth. "It wasn't just the money that appealed to him. It was the image of himself going into a bank holding a gun, knowing that he had complete power over those he was robbing." Barnes also writes that Kathryn not only helped in the planning of these robberies, but that she dressed like a man and participated as an armed getaway driver during some of them.

Kathryn also had an image of her husband, and she began spreading the word among her bootlegging customers and associates that her man was a brutal, efficient bank robber. To prove the point, she gave him a second-hand Thompson machine gun, model 1921, serial number 4907, and insisted that he practice with it while visiting at the Shannon farm near Paradise, Texas. She bought it from J. Kar, a pawnbroker at the Wolfe & Klar Pawn Shop in Fort Worth that was the southwest distributor for Colt's Arms Manufacturing Company, and paid two hundred fifty dollars for it. According to William Helmer, author of http://www.amazon.com/Public-Enemies-Americas-Criminal-1919-

*Public
Enemies: America's Criminal Past, 1919-1940,*
"Wolfe & Klar was also the source of guns for Hyman
Lebman in San Antonio who was converting them
into full automatics for bank robber and murderer
Baby Face Nelson, a name given to him because of
his youthful appearance and small stature, and his
partner, John Dillinger, known for having robbed
twenty-four banks and four police stations." Both
would be named on FBI Director Hoover's "Public
Enemy No. 1" list.

Kathryn was an expert shot with most types of guns,
according to the FBI, including the hand guns, shot
guns, rifles, and the "Tommy" gun. It has been
reported that George could also handle the "chopper"
(or "Chicago typewriter," as the big city mobsters
called it), and named his Tommy gun "the Little
Stenog" because he could "write his name on the
side of a barn" by shooting bullets.

Kathryn continued promoting "the Big Guy" in Fort
Worth dives, dumps, and hangouts, bragging that
"Machine Gun Kelly" was so expert with his weapon
that he could pop walnuts off the top of a fence at
thirty feet, and passing out his spent brass shell
casings as souvenirs.

Machine Gun Kelly would make his own self-serving
statements, saying that he "liked to use a machine
gun at close range without the stock, with the butt
against his hip." He also bragged that he "spent

twenty-five to thirty dollars a week on slugs so he could practice." He was known for carrying a large bag with him that concealed two machine guns, the one Kathryn bought for him, and another one, also a 1921 model, 45 caliber, serial number 4685.

There is little doubt that these stories have been embellished over the years. For one thing, Kelly was never keen on fire arms. For another, it has been pointed out that pecan trees are dominant in the area rather than walnut trees. There is also some question as to whether it was Kathryn who actually came up with the name "Machine Gun Kelly." The FBI had its own ubiquitous public relations arm which cleverly played up the frightening nickname while seeking Kelly; thereby painting Hoover and his agents as heroic and courageous in their pursuit of this extremely dangerous, heavily armed public enemy. The FBI's wanted poster warned that Kelly was an "expert machine gunner," while at the same time some of the bureau's press releases labeled him "a desperate character."

Other stories spread around the Southwest of the fearless robber calling himself "Machine Gun Kelly," a deadly master of the Tommy gun, who "signed" his holdups by blasting his name across billboards and bank walls. There was one incident where, following a bank robbery in Texas, Kelly used his machine gun to shoot his last name on a signpost as he and Kathryn raced out of town, but this one act wouldn't justify newspapers of the day proclaiming Kelly "the most dangerous man in America." More than likely it was just bad timing for Kelly. The fact is, Kelly never killed anyone—or, as far as anyone knows, even fired his weapon in anger.

Kelly's list of underworld associates continued to grow. He became acquainted with Chicago mobsters and "Kid Cann," operated by Isadore Blumenfeld, a Jewish-American organized crime figure based in Minneapolis, Minnesota. Kelly's accomplices on various crimes included Eddie Bentz, who would boast to the FBI of having robbed between "fifty and a hundred banks" in his life; Edward Doll, alias Eddie "Blackie" LaRue or "Burlington Eddie," known for bootlegging, bank robbery, and kidnapping, and alleged to be a "spot killer" for Chicago mobsters; and Albert L. Bates, whose aliases include George Bates, George L. Davis, George Harris and J.B. King, wanted for bank robberies across the country and suspected of murdering his accomplices, J.E. "Mike" Conway and Frank "Frisco Whitey" Carroll.

Kelly continued to work with Keating, Holden and others until early 1932 when he began working with Albert L. Bates. Bates had an arrest record dating back to March 1916 when he was convicted of burglary and sentenced from one to fifteen years in the state penitentiary at Carson City, Nevada. Paroled a year and a half later, his next sentence was a six-month stretch for petty theft in Salt Lake City. In August 1921, Bates received another sentence for burglary in the Utah State Penitentiary.

He escaped in October, 1926, but less than seven months later he was serving a three-to-five year burglary sentence in Colorado. After his release in July 1930, Bates made his way to the Midwest and spent thirty days in jail on a minor charge in Michigan. Bates and Kelly would work together for more than a year.

According to Allan May, author and organized crime historian, Kelly's first kidnapping occurred in 1930 with a former Cicero, Illinois police officer named Bernard "Big Phil" Phillips. "Tall, husky, and slow-spoken, Phillips had been fired as a traffic cop for extortion. During the kidnapping, one of the victims taken by Phillips was killed when Phillips' gun accidentally discharged."

Later, Phillips asked Kelly to join him in another kidnapping, but Kelly declined, concluding that the proposed victim did not have enough money to pay the ransom. Phillips went ahead with the abduction but soon discovered that Kelly's assessment had been correct. Phillips then released the victim with the ridiculous order to bring his own ransom to a meeting. In attempting to collect the ransom, he borrowed Kelly's Cadillac, thus making Kelly the suspect for Philips' crime. Because he was being hunted, Kelly had to flee to Chicago with his Cadillac coupe loaded into the back end of a truck.

Kelly's second kidnapping attempt, along with his partner, bootlegger and car thief Eddie Doll, took place on January 27, 1932. Howard Woolverton, a

South Bend, Indiana, banker, was returning home with his wife when a gunman jumped on the running board of their car and forced his way into the automobile. After ordering Woolverton to drive out of town, they stopped two miles outside the city where Woolverton was forced into another car that had been following them. Mrs. Woolverton was then given a ransom note demanding fifty thousand dollars. After driving Woolverton around the northern part of Indiana for two days, the victim was finally able to convince Kelly and Doll that he didn't have the money to pay the ransom. He was released just outside Michigan City, Indiana, on his promise to raise the money. Calls and letters to his home demanding the money were ignored, however, and eventually his kidnappers stopped trying to contact him.

Not discouraged, Kathryn and George made plans for still another kidnapping, this one involving Guy Waggoner, the son of a Fort Worth oil magnate. Kathryn had a party at their Mulkey Street home and invited Fort Worth police detectives K.W. Swinney and Ed Weatherford. Believing they were corrupt, Kathryn talked to them about taking part in the kidnapping. Swinney and Weatherford, however, knowing of the Kellys' criminal history, were trying to cultivate Kathryn into becoming an informant. They declined, telling her it was too risky.

Before the detectives left, she asked them for a favor: If Kelly or his partner Bates were ever arrested in another state, could the detectives be counted on to contact that authority and claim they were wanted in Texas for bank robbery? "And you boys come and claim them," meaning the detectives would then allow them to escape from custody. "Is that a go?" she asked. Swinney and Weatherford assured her they would. The detectives then contacted the FBI who placed the oilman's son under constant police surveillance. With so many police around the young man, the Kellys dropped their plan to kidnap him.

Kelly, like a number of other criminals during that era of Prohibition, saw kidnapping as a relatively safe, easy way to get a lot of money fast. Basically, it involved identifying a wealthy victim, finding a safe, hidden place to keep the victim, and working out a plan to collect the ransom. A kidnapping was less dangerous than robbing a bank, Kathryn and George reasoned, and they could collect whatever they demanded. Whereas, in a bank robbery, the take was uncertain, especially since they were in the midst of the Great Depression when even the banks occasionally ran short of cash. While the Kellys considered their next move, several unrelated events occurred which the FBI and law enforcement agencies in the Midwest would incorrectly tie into the Kelly legend.

First, Kelly's former Leavenworth associate and one-time bank-robbing partner, Harvey Bailey, had been arrested and incarcerated in the state penitentiary in

Lansing, Kansas. On May 30, 1933, Bailey, Wilbur Underhill and nine others, using guns allegedly smuggled into the prison by Frank Nash, kidnapped the warden and two prison guards in a daring escape. The hostages were later released unharmed. After regrouping in the Cookson Hills of eastern Oklahoma, Bailey and Underhill would lead a gang which pulled off several bank robberies in that state.

The second event was the June 17, 1933, Kansas City Massacre—also referred to as the Union Station Massacre. Verne Miller, a freelance Prohibition gunman, bootlegger, bank robber, and former sheriff in Huron, South Dakota, and two unidentified accomplices attempted to free Nash from a group of federal agents and law enforcement officers. Nash, who had been arrested by federal agents in Hot Springs, Arkansas, the day before, was being transferred back to Leavenworth. During this ill-fated rescue attempt five people—four law officers and Nash—were killed. Years later it would be revealed that Nash and at least two of the law officers died from friendly fire.

Although the FBI would incorrectly name gangsters "Pretty Boy" Floyd, a bank robber who operated primarily in the Midwest and West South Central States, and Adam "Eddie" Richetti, bank robber and kidnapper, as the accomplices months later, initial suspects included Kelly, Bailey and Underhill.

In that same month, Tulsa's Barker-Karpis gang, comprised of Ma "Arrie" Barker and her sons and the gang of Alvin Karpis, abducted beer baron William A. Hamm at St. Paul. They demanded a one hundred thousand dollar ransom. Hamm was taken to Wisconsin, where he was forced to sign four ransom notes. Then he was moved to a hideout in Bensenville, Illinois, and held prisoner until the kidnappers had been paid. Once the money was handed over, Hamm was released unharmed near Wyoming, Minnesota. Albert Bates would later claim that Ma Barker couldn't even organize breakfast, much less "a job." However, history would prove otherwise.

While the search had gone on for Hamm's abductors, other prominent citizens fell victim to kidnapping: An Atlanta banker was taken in an unsuccessful effort to get forty thousand dollars in ransom; John J. O'Connell, Jr., the twenty-four-year-old son and nephew of several New York politicians, was kidnapped and two hundred fifty thousand dollars demanded for his return of which only forty thousand dollars was paid; August Luer, an Alton, Illinois banker, was abducted and then released without receiving the demanded one hundred thousand dollars.

On learning of these kidnappings and some of the successful payoffs, despite their own lackluster track record in kidnapping, the Kellys and Bates soon decided on yet another attempt. This one was destined to firmly set George Ramsey Kelly's name— aka George Barnes, George Kelly, J.J. Rosenburg, and George Celino Barnes—into the annals of crime history.

# CHAPTER 4

## The Urschel Kidnapping

As Kathryn poured over the newspaper society pages in search for their next victim, she read about Charles Urschel recently being married to Berenice Slick, the widow of oil magnate, "King of the Wildcatters," Tom Slick. Their combined fortunes created one of the wealthiest couples in Oklahoma City. With their new victim now identified, Kathryn, George, and Albert Bates began planning the intricate details of their next kidnapping.

Charles F. Urschel started out as an Ohio farm boy, born in Hancock County on March 7, 1890, served in the Army stateside during World War I, and put together enough cash to try his luck in the Oklahoma oil fields. He married Flored Slick and became the trusted business partner of her brother, Tom Slick, in 1919 following the discovery of the Cushing oilfield, which at that time accounted for seventeen percent of the United States and three percent of world production of oil. Tom died of a massive stroke during surgery in August 1930, and Flored died a year later. Charles then married Slick's widow and moved into her Oklahoma City 6,330 square foot mansion that had been built in 1923. Considered one of the wealthiest couples in Oklahoma City, they had hired an armed bodyguard, but later fired him for sleeping on the job.

On July 22, 1933, Charles and Berenice were entertaining their friends, Walter R. Jarrett and his wife, Clyde, in a rubber of bridge when George Kelly and Albert Bates entered the front porch of the home, located at 327 N.W. 18th Street in the exclusive Heritage Hills district of Oklahoma City. Bates carried a hand gun, and Kelly, who was armed with a machine gun, demanded to know which man was Urschel. When neither man spoke up, both were taken and forced into the back seat of a Chevrolet sedan.

Kelly drove a few miles out of town before stopping. Both men were searched for identification. In addition to his identification, Jarrett had fifty-one dollars which was taken. He was then released with enough money for cab fare. He later told officials that the "tall man" (eventually identified as Kelly) was constantly addressed by his companion as

"Floyd" and guessed that this was an attempt to make them think the kidnap leader was "Pretty Boy" Floyd.

Urschel, who was given ear plugs and blindfolded, was driven across two states to the Shannon ranch in Texas, but not without a few hitches along the way that would give the phrase "comedy of errors" a whole new meaning. Since the getaway driver—presumably Kelly—forgot to put gas in the car before the kidnapping, the party was stranded for an hour while someone went to get gas. By then it had started to rain, and the car got stuck in the mud, thereby requiring one of the men to push it. Once back on the way, the driver fell asleep, ran the car into a ditch, and then had to ask a farmer for directions that would eventually take them to the hideout where Urschel was finally placed under guard by Kathryn's stepfather, "Boss" Shannon, and his son, Armon, known as "Potatoes." This was after they attempted to hide Urschel at Ma Coleman's, Kathryn's grandmother, who created such a fuss for being disturbed in the middle of the night that the kidnappers had to take their victim to Boss Shannon's house. Armon was promised fifteen hundred dollars by George for agreeing to help. Boss, according to Bruce Barnes, and to Boss's own sworn testimony, participated through intimidation. Even though George had never killed anyone, Boss didn't want to be the first.

Within five minutes of the abduction, Berenice Urschel had already called first a federal judge, the local police, then the direct line of Director J. Edgar Hoover at NAtional 8-7117 in Washington, D.C., in accordance with the instructions given by Director Hoover to the general public in a *Time* magazine article regarding the wave of kidnappings that had taken place across the country. Even though it was midnight, it was Director Hoover himself who took the call.

The FBI, then known as the Division of Investigation, took charge of the case immediately. Not only did they need to capture the perpetrators as quickly as possible, this new division in the government's arm of law needed to demonstrate its effectiveness in the Department of Justice's fight against crime. When Franklin Delano Roosevelt became president in March 1933 it seemed likely that J. Edgar Hoover would be fired. However, with the passage of the Lindbergh Law, the war on crime became a mass media event that provided Hoover with opportunities to elevate his authority and his celebrity, eventually making him the main character in the battle between G-men and gangsters. In addition, Charles Urschel wasn't just a wealthy Oklahoma oilman and prominent citizen; he was a personal friend of President Franklin Delano Roosevelt.

The special agents heading up the Division of Investigation offices in San Antonio and Dallas, additional agents from Dallas and El Paso, and all but one agent in the Oklahoma City office were ordered to work on the Urschel case. This was the first gangland kidnapping under the new Federal Kidnapping Law Act, 18 U.S.C. § 1201, and Hoover wanted to set an example by taking personal charge, determined to catch the "dirty yellow rats" responsible.

Based on what the disheveled Jarrett had been able to tell the agents once he made his way back to the Urschel residence, they knew the kidnappers had driven south. The next day newspapers across the country carried the story of the wealthy oil man's abduction.

Once the kidnapping became known, numerous letters and telephone calls were received, many of which were anonymous, indicating possible leads. Even though few were of value, all had to be followed. There was some speculation that Elizabeth Slick, the daughter of Berenice and her late husband, Tom Slick, may have been the original target of the kidnappers. When the kidnappers were described by Mrs. Urschel and the Jarretts to the police, Elizabeth recalled seeing two men fitting those descriptions following her only days earlier. It is believed that there were other possibilities considered as well, including a Texas banker, a Missouri brewer, and two Oklahomans, one a bank president, and the other a dry goods merchant.

As the day wore on, the family and police agreed that it would be good strategy for Mrs. Urschel to issue a statement to the large congregation of reporters, photographers, newsreel cameramen, and others now camped near the Urschel home. In her statement, Mrs. Urschel said:

*… I am in no way interested in your capture or prosecution. I care only for the safe return of my husband. To facilitate this I have had police withdrawn from my house, and there is no one here now except our family…. We have made preliminary arrangements to negotiate with you speedily and confidentially. Arthur Seeligson, my husband's closest friend, will be in charge. You can trust him. The welfare of my husband, and his immediate return, is my only concern.*

The fact that law enforcement officers would remain on the premises would be carefully covered up throughout the crisis, as would the onslaught of what Agent Colvin called "nut notes and chiseling propositions" that flooded in—fake calls, letters, and wires from cranks, extortionists, psychics, and demented hoaxers, all expecting a reward for information they could provide. In one instance, Mrs. Urschel slipped out of the house with one thousand dollars and had a friend to drive her, as she lay hidden on the floorboard in the backseat, to a secret meeting with an "informant," even though she had been advised by the FBI not to. The informant took the money and disappeared, giving Mrs. Urschel no information.

The next afternoon, Urschel, Kelly and Bates arrived at the Shannon's 500-acre ranch in Paradise, Texas, which was owned by Kathryn's stepfather, "Boss" Shannon. Urschel, still blindfolded, was kept in the garage until after dark. He was then led into the house and up some stairs into a room where he was given a pair of Kelly's pajamas to wear and chained to an iron bed. Cotton was stuffed in his ears and taped over. The following morning, Urschel's captors read the headlines to him regarding the kidnapping over breakfast. That evening he was moved to a small tenant shack where Boss Shannon's son, Armon, lived with his young pregnant wife, Oletha, and their fourteen-month-old infant daughter, Ora Maudene. He was handcuffed to a baby's highchair and slept on a quilt placed on the floor.

Two days following Urschel's abduction, in a feeble attempt to establish an alibi, Kathryn contacted Weatherford and Swinney, the two Fort Worth detectives she had entertained at the party in her Mulkey Street home earlier to ask what they knew about the case and if there were any leads. It was only curiosity on her part, she said, and then explained she'd been "back east" visiting friends in St. Louis. One of the detectives, however, noticed an Oklahoma newspaper headlining the kidnapping on her car seat. He also noticed that her car's sidewalls were caked with red mud common to the farmland in that area and determined that the car was registered to an Ora Shannon of Paradise, Texas. He passed on his observations and suspicions to his superiors, who in turn relayed them to the FBI. When they showed a mug shot of Kelly to Mrs. Urschel, she immediately identified him.

What Charles Urschel's kidnappers did not realize about their victim was that he had keen powers of observation and a photogenic memory. During the nine days he was held captive, he noted that twice each day he could hear airplanes fly over. When he did, he would wait a few minutes, then ask his captors what time it was. He was able to determine that the times were at 9:45 a.m. and 5:45 p.m. He noted a distinct mineral taste to the water he drank from a tin cup, drawn from a well by a rope and bucket on a pulley which made considerable noise. He also planted his fingerprints on everything he could touch, counted footsteps when moved from place to place, and made mental notes of the smells and various sounds he heard—farm animals, rain falling—things he would provide in a full report to the FBI for their later use.

Urschel was treated well, according to his own testimony, as the gang waited for the two hundred thousand dollar ransom, the largest ever paid in American history. When the kidnappers were absent, Boss took over as the main guard, assisted from time to time by Armon, who played the violin for Urschel a couple of evenings. Slowly, a cordial, if not somewhat strained, relationship developed between the men as Urschel attempted to find subjects of common interest. Discussions soon turned toward their mutual enjoyment of hunting with dogs, fishing, and tracking deer and game birds.

The conversations he had with the kidnappers were somewhat revealing in other ways as well. In one talk with Bates, the outlaw said of Bonnie and Clyde, "They're just a couple of cheap filling station and car thieves.... I've been stealing for twenty-five years and my group doesn't deal in anything cheap. I wouldn't hesitate to rob the Security National Bank."

Bonnie Elizabeth Parker and Clyde Chestnut Barrow, aka Clyde Champion Barrow, were outlaws and robbers from the Dallas area who traveled the central United States with their gang. Believed to have killed at least nine police officers and several civilians, their exploits also included a dozen or so bank robberies; but it was common knowledge that Barrow preferred to rob small stores or rural gas stations. The couple were eventually ambushed and killed near the town of Sailes, in Bienville Parish, Louisiana, by law officers.

Bates also admitted that he and his partner had committed several bank robberies and had declined the invitation to help rob a Clinton, Iowa, bank, because "the escape road out of town wasn't safe enough."

Kelly was just as talkative, and he told Urschel, "This place is as safe as it can be," referring to the Shannon ranch. "All the boys use it. After they pull a bank job or something they come down here to cool off."

Urschel remembered everything that was said, including that the area had recently suffered a severe drought, something he had overheard when they had stopped for gas outside of Paradise, Texas. "The crops around here are burned up," the female gas station attendant said when one of the kidnappers asked, "although we may make some broom corn."

There are various stories regarding the request for the ransom money, but it has been suggested by author John Toland in his book, *The Dillinger Days,* that "it was Urschel who came up with the idea that they contact a family friend in Tulsa, John G. Catlett, when Kelly expressed concern over there being so many federal agents in Oklahoma City, making it difficult to contact his family there." Urschel was given some paper and a pencil and told to write two notes:  one to Catlett, and one to Mrs. Urschel. The following morning, a messenger delivered an envelope to the Catlett home that contained three letters. The letter to Catlett urged him not to discuss the matter with anyone other than those mentioned. The second letter was for Urschel's wife.  The third was addressed to E.E. Kirkpatrick, another friend of the family and brother-in-law to Mrs. Urschel through her late husband.

The letter to Kirkpatrick, a newspaperman, rancher, and oilman was handed to him after he was called out to the Urschel home. It was a ransom demand asking for two hundred thousand dollars in genuine used federal reserve currency in the denomination of twenty dollar ($20.00) bills. The note continued:

*… It will be useless for you to attempt taking notes of serial numbers making up dummy package, or anything else in the line of attempted double cross. Bear this in mind, Charles F. Urschel will remain in our custody until money has been inspected and exchanged and furthermore will be at the scene of contact for pay-off and if there should be any attempt at any double XX it will be he that suffers the consequence.*

*RUN THIS AD FOR ONE WEEK IN DAILY OKLAHOMAN.*

*'FOR SALE – 160 Acres Land, good five room house, deep well. Also Cows, Tools, Tractor, Corn, and Hay. $3750.00 for quick sale… TERMS… Box # _____ '*

The ad was placed as instructed in Thursday's editions and assigned Box No. 807, and on July 28, an envelope addressed to the *Daily Oklahoman* was received. It was from Joplin, Missouri, and it contained a letter to Kirkpatrick with additional instructions:

*… You will pack two hundred thousand dollars ($200,000) in used genuine federal reserve notes of twenty dollar denomination in a suitable light colored*

*leather bag and have some-one purchase transportation for you, including berth, aboard Train #28 (The Sooner) which departs at 10:10 p.m. via the M.K. & T. Lines for Kansas City, Mo.*

*You will ride on the observation platform where you may be observed by someone at some Station along the Line between Okla. City and K.C. Mo. If indications are alright, somewhere along the Right-of-Way you will observe a Fire on the Right Side of Track (Facing direction train is bound) that first Fire will be your Cue to be prepared to throw BAG to Track immediately after passing SECOND FIRE.*

*REMEMBER THIS – IF ANY TRICKERY IS ATTEMPTED YOU WILL FIND THE REMAINS OF URSCHEL AND INSTEAD OF JOY THERE WILL BE DOUBLE GRIEF – FOR, SOME-ONE VERY NEAR AND DEAR TO THE URSCHEL FAMILY IS UNDER CONSTANT SURVEILLANCE AND WILL LIKE-WISE SUFFER FOR YOUR ERROR.*

The note then concluded:

*If there is the slightest HITCH in these PLANS for any reason what-so-ever, not your fault, you will proceed on into Kansas City, Mo. And register at the Muehlebach Hotel under the name of E.E. Kincaid of Little Rock, Arkansas and await further instructions there.*

*THE MAIN THING IS DO NOT DIVULGE THE CONTENTS OF THIS LETTER TO ANY LAW*

*AUTHORITIES FOR WE HAVE NO INTENTION OF FURTHER COMMUNICATION.*

*YOU ARE TO MAKE THIS TRIP SATURDAY JULY 29TH 1933....*

The FBI obtained the two hundred thousand dollars in used twenty dollar notes of the Federal Reserve Bank, Tenth District, and the serial numbers were recorded. The money was placed in a new, light-colored leather Gladstone bag, according to the instructions, but at the same time, fearing an attempt at high jacking, another identical bag was purchased and filled with old magazines.

As an additional precaution and deliberately going against the instructions, it was decided that Catlett would accompany Kirkpatrick to Kansas City. By prearrangement, Catlett sat just inside the rear of the observation car, while Kirkpatrick sat on the observation platform with the bag containing the magazines. No signals were observed, and Kirkpatrick remained on the platform all night, riding there all the way to Kansas City.

Once in Kansas City, Kirkpatrick and Catlett immediately went to the Muehlebach Hotel where Kirkpatrick registered as E.E. Kincaid. In his book *To Right a Wrong*, Bruce Barnes claims that his father and Bates actually boarded the train at Arcadia, Kansas, and grew suspicious when they saw Catlett was with Kirkpatrick. It has also been reported that Kathryn was on the train as well. However, Kelly in his note had told Kirkpatrick that if anything went wrong, he was to check into the Muehlebach Hotel in Kansas City.

Once in his room, Kirkpatrick received a telegram from Tulsa, Oklahoma, as follows: "Owing to unavoidable incident unable to keep appointed. Will phone you about six. Signed, C.H. Moore."

About 5:30 p.m., on Sunday, July 30, Kirkpatrick received a telephone call from someone claiming to be Moore who then instructed Kirkpatrick to take a taxicab to the LaSalle Hotel and walk west a block or two. Kirkpatrick asked if a friend could accompany him, to which came the reply, "Hell, no! We know all about your friend. You come alone and unarmed." Kirkpatrick stuck an automatic in his belt, put on his hat, and picked up the Gladstone bag containing the money. "Godspeed and good luck," said Catlett.

Kirkpatrick reached the LaSalle Hotel within minutes and leisurely walked west along Linwood Boulevard no more than a block before he was approached by a man with black hair and dark skin, wearing a stylish summer suit, two-toned shoes, and a turned-down Panama hat. Kirkpatrick would later identify the man as Machine Gun Kelly as well as the two ransom notes addressed to him—Government Exhibits 12 and 55.

At first Kirkpatrick stalled when Kelly demanded the bag, asking when Urschel would be home. He put the bag on the sidewalk between his legs. "Tell me definitely what I can tell Mrs. Urschel," he said.

Red-faced and nervous, muttering they were being watched, Kelly told Kirkpatrick to return to the hotel, and promised that Urschel would be home within twelve hours. Kirkpatrick left the bag and walked away. He returned to the hotel and from there he proceeded to Oklahoma City. Catlett returned to Tulsa.

On the afternoon of July 31, Bates and Kelly returned to the Shannon ranch with the ransom money. After whooping it up over their success, they got down to the business of dividing the money. The two men each gave Harvey Bailey five hundred dollars, supposedly to settle an old debt. Bailey had shown up at the ranch a few days earlier, borrowed Kelly's machine gun to rob a bank in Kingfisher, Oklahoma, on August 9, then returned to the ranch to recover from a leg wound he suffered during his prison escape.

There was some discussion over the fate of Urschel, and it has been reported that Kathryn wanted to "kill the bastard." In the end, however, they decided it was best to release him unharmed; otherwise it might be bad for future business, Kelly reasoned. Urschel was told he could clean up and shave off his nine-day beard. They furnished him with a small, cracked and cloudy hand mirror, and an old straight-edge razor, some shaving cream, a brush, and a basin of water. He was also given a brand new short-sleeve sport shirt and an ill-fitting straw hat to wear on the return ride home.

On Monday, July 31, two cars left the Shannon ranch, one car with Urschel and the other a lead car. Even though it is less than two hundred miles from Paradise to Oklahoma City, the journey took about eight hours until at last they arrived at a place near Norman, Oklahoma, twenty miles outside of Oklahoma City. Urschel was given back his watch along with ten dollars and released.

Urschel walked through the drizzling rain to a filling station/barbecue stand called Classen's and called a cab. Sometime between 9:00 and 11:00 p.m. on July 31, Urschel arrived back at his home exhausted, having had very little sleep over the nine days of captivity. Adding insult to injury, the officer guarding his front door refused to let Urschel in, not recognizing him and hardly expecting the victim to ride up in a taxicab wearing a sport shirt and straw hat. Urschel retreated to the back door and let himself into his own house. FBI Agent Gus Jones, formerly from Texas and assigned to the case by J. Edgar Hoover two days after Charles Urschel's abduction, arrived at the Urschel home less than thirty minutes later eager to debrief the victim. However, Urschel was too exhausted. The next morning, rested and determined to catch the people responsible for his abduction, Urschel gave Agent Jones his full, detailed statement of the entire incident.

# CHAPTER 5

## The Investigation

U rschel's statement to the FBI was comprehensive. In addition to the things he remembered once they arrived at the location where he was held, he remembered things en route, such as the car passing through oil fields about an hour after his abduction—possibly a small field or the end of a large one. He could smell the gas and hear the oil pumps working. He remembered driving through two gates, and then stopping so the license plate from the Chevrolet sedan could be transferred to a larger car, possibly a seven-passenger Cadillac or Buick. Urschel stated that about 9 or 10 a.m. it rained and the road became slippery, so much so that one of the men had to get out and push the car.

When they arrived at their destination, Urschel asked for the time. It was 2:30 p.m. They remained in what Urschel assumed was some sort of garage until dark when he was taken outside, through a narrow gate and along a boardwalk. He was then led into a house and into a room with two beds. He heard the voices of a man and woman in an adjoining room, but they soon left. He ate at a small table and heard barnyard animals outside.

The next day, he was taken in an automobile by the two men to another house about 15 minutes driving distance. At this house—a crude shack—he was told to lie on some blankets in a corner of the room. His observations included among other things a banging screen door, three small rooms and their dimensions, two small porches, the direction of the bare floorboards, a potbellied wood cook stove, a blue high chair, an old-fashioned organ, a hole in the door where a knob had once been, a missing front window pane filled with a piece of cardboard, and the shack itself, "infested," as he put it, "with rats."

He also heard the voices of a man and woman. Besides the two men who kidnapped him, Urschel stated that he was also guarded by an old man and a younger man. Later, a chain was attached to his handcuffs which allowed him to move about to some extent. He observed dogs, chickens, cows, a mule, and hogs around the place and was told by one of the guards that they had four milk cows. Having grown up on a farm, it was easy for him to identify the animals. Also, he had determined that a plane would always pass over at approximately 9:45 in the morning and then again at 5:45 in the evening. However, on Sunday, July 30, when it rained very hard, the morning plane did not pass.

A review of all airplane schedules within a radius of 600 miles of Oklahoma City was made, and the records of the meteorologist of the United States Weather Bureau of Dallas, Texas, were consulted. It was determined that a plane normally leaving Fort Worth at 11:45 a.m. had been detained by a storm on Sunday, July 30, and subsequently had taken a northerly course to avoid the storm.

With air travel being relatively rare back then, it didn't take long for the agents to figure that Paradise was on the flight path between Fort Worth and Amarillo. Also, the records of the meteorologist indicated that Paradise and vicinity had an extremely dry season, causing the corn to burn in June; and that the first real rain since May 20 in that vicinity was on July 30.

While no effort was made by the FBI to apprehend the kidnappers until after the release of Urschel, as early as July 24, two days after Urschel was kidnapped, it had been disclosed that Kathryn's mother and stepfather lived on a ranch near Paradise, and that Kathryn and George Kelly had been seen in the area during the period in question. Based on the information that had already been provided by the two Fort Worth detectives,

Weatherford and Swinney, there had been an on-going nationwide search for the Kellys. Several years later, gangster Alvin Karpis, one of the three leaders of the Barker-Karpis gang and the last "Public Enemy No.1" to be taken, told former FBI agent Tom McDade a different version of how the Urschel case was solved: "There were two local cops in on it and when they didn't get their split, they blew the whistle." It is assumed he was referring to Weatherford and Swinney.

With the information Urschel supplied, the FBI was able to locate the Shannon ranch. On August 10, FBI Special Agent Edward Dowd drove to the Shannon ranch and posed as an inspector. After spending time there, he drove the short distance to Armon's house. There he was able to identify all of the things Urschel had remembered, including the squeaky well pulley. Dowd asked for a drink of water and experienced the mineral taste for himself.

Ten days after Urschel's release on August 12, fourteen men—four federal agents, four Dallas detectives, four Fort Worth detectives, including Weatherford and Swinney, a deputy sheriff from Oklahoma City, and Charles Urschel, armed with his own sawed-off shotgun—surrounded the farm of Ora and Boss Shannon. Urschel insisted on going along because he wanted to see the place for himself as well as the people who had kept him hostage.

Boss Shannon was the first to surrender after one of the agents called out his name. He was followed by his wife, Ora. Agent Dowd noticed a man sleeping on a cot in the yard with a machine gun on the ground next to him, and when Shannon identified him as Harvey Bailey, he, too, was arrested. Dowd later put in his report:

*... Special Agent in Charge Jones rushed over with a machine gun and put it close to Bailey's head.... On the bed alongside of Bailey was a fully loaded 331 Winchester Automatic Rifle and a Colts .45 Automatic Pistol.... Bailey had been sleeping in his BVDs and his pants and shirt were at the foot of the bed. In Bailey's pants were found $1,200.00 in paper money, $700.00 of which consisted of $20.00 bills, being part of the ransom money paid by Charles F. Urschel.*

There are different versions of where Bailey was actually captured. A newspaper report had him on a small cot inside the house. Author John Toland described him sleeping on a bed in the back yard, while historian Rick Mattix had Bailey sleeping on the porch. All accounts, however, described him as being well armed, and the headlines in newspapers across the country proclaimed the Kansas City Massacre chief had been apprehended.

Agent Gus Jones later testified that Bailey told him he'd only had the machine gun four days but knew that it had previously been used by Kansas City gangsters in the murder of a hoodlum named Ferris Anthon when he attempted to challenge the Kansas City crime family. The FBI subsequently traced the gun to the Fort Worth pawnshop where Kathryn had bought it. There were later allegations that Kathryn bought several machine guns that were shipped to Chicago and stored for the Kellys at the Janitors' Union run by Louis "Two-Gun" Alterie, aka "Diamond Jack Alterie," a notorious hitman for the Chicago North Side Gang. It was yet another story to perpetuate the Machine Gun Kelly image, substantiated by Justice Department press releases describing Kelly as a "desperate character" who had served "several prison sentences," an "expert machine gunner," and a leader of "one of the most feared gangs in the Southwest."

After arresting Boss and Ora Shannon and Harvey Bailey, the officers then went to Armon's house and arrested him and his wife, Oletha. Armon was ready to tell what little he knew, even though Ora yelled at him to "Keep your mouth shut. Don't tell them a damned thing." He went on, however, to say that a pair of armed kidnappers had forced him to keep their prisoner in his dwelling and help his father stand watch over him. "They brought Mr. Urschel here…. They made me do it, Kelly and Bates." So now the officers knew the identities of both kidnappers. Berenice Urschel and Walter Jarrett had already identified Kelly's mug shots, and now Armon had given them the name of the other kidnapper, a petty criminal by the name of Albert Bates, aka J.B. King or George L. Davis.

Urschel was able to identify the house of Boss and Ora Shannon as the place he was first held, and that of Armon Shannon as the house where he was kept until his release. Urschel also identified Boss and Armon Shannon by their voices as the men who stood guard over him during the absence of the two kidnappers. He was able to identify other things as well, including the residences by the number of steps it had taken him to enter, the baby's chair where he had been handcuffed, the galvanized bucket and tin cup, the squeaking well pulley, and the farm animals around the two houses.

At first vehemently denying any knowledge of the crime, Boss Shannon later confirmed what "Potatoes" had already admitted; that Urschel had been held at their homes, and that they had stood guard over him. Boss, however, went on to state that Urschel had been kidnapped by George Kelly and Albert Bates; and if he hadn't help guard Urschel, Kelly had threatened to kill him.

Boss and Ora Shannon, Armon "Potatoes" and Oletha Brown Shannon, and Harvey Bailey were taken to the FBI Dallas office where all but Bailey and Oletha made statements admitting their participation in the crime. Oletha would later be released on the failure of the grand jury to indict. Boss Shannon placed full blame for the entire episode on George Kelly and Albert Bates and claimed that Bailey had nothing to do with the kidnapping, explaining that he had only come to spend the night at the ranch. However, Shannon's explanation was disregarded.

The Shannons and Bailey were booked into the Dallas County jail, with Bailey placed in solitary confinement under a false name to avoid publicity about his arrest. That same afternoon, Albert L. Bates was taken into custody in Denver, Colorado, on the suspicion of passing stolen checks. At the time of his arrest, he had in his possession six hundred sixty dollars, later identified by Bureau agents as part of the Urschel ransom money. He also had a machine gun. He was immediately transported to Dallas to stand trial for the kidnapping. Seven other people were arrested in the Minneapolis-St. Paul area for passing ransom money. More arrests were soon to follow.

# CHAPTER 6

## The Pursuit

After burying part of their share of the ransom money on other farms near the Shannon ranch, the Kellys and Bates had left the Shannon ranch a few days earlier in Kathryn's sixteen-cylinder Cadillac, which Kathryn had named "Sweet Sixteen," with the bulk of the ransom money. Confident they were not suspected in the Urschel kidnapping, they drove to Minneapolis where they sold a portion of the ransom money before splitting up.

On August 5, the Kellys left the Twin Cities just before FBI agents, alerted to the fact that twenty dollar bills with serial numbers fitting the ransom money were discovered in that area, made their first arrests in the kidnapping case. The men arrested were Minneapolis crime boss Isadore Kid Cann Blumenfeld and his men, Sam Kronick, Sam Kizberg, Edward Barney Berman, and Clifford Skelly. Eventually, only Berman and Skelly would be convicted of passing ransom money.

On learning of the arrests and that they had been identified, Kathryn and George would eventually flee through at least sixteen states—Arkansas, Colorado, Illinois, Indiana, Iowa, Kansas, Kentucky, Minnesota, Missouri, New York, Ohio, Oklahoma, Pennsylvania, Tennessee, Texas, and Wisconsin—even into Mexico, according to Bruce Barnes, trading cars along the way, implicating friends and relatives, and adopting various disguises including dressing as tramps. Kathryn wore a red wig which she paid eighty dollars for, and Kelly dyed his hair, first red, then bright yellow. Both were drinking heavily, and for a while, they split up. At some point, Kathryn returned to her Fort Worth home where her friend, Louise Magness, was staying.

Ironically, police received a tip about another kidnap plot against Guy Waggoner, the Fort Worth oilman's son. Waggoner had a summer home in Broadmoor, Colorado, a suburb of Colorado Springs where the young Waggoner was staying. Once again he was placed under guard. The plotters of the kidnapping were alleged to be Machine Gun Kelly, Albert Bates, and Verne Miller, the actual perpetrator of the Kansas City Massacre.

In Chicago, a man named Frank Kristoff was arrested with several hundred dollars' worth of stolen money orders that had been taken in the 1932 Tupelo, Mississippi, bank robbery. Kristoff claimed to have gotten them from a man named "Joe" at a restaurant in Denver, and he identified "Joe" from a mug shot as Albert Bates.

On the same day the Shannons and Bailey were arrested in Texas, Bates was picked up at a hotel run by ex-convict Herman Herbert at 19th and Arapahoe in Denver. Claiming to be George L. Davis, but later admitting his true identity, he had six hundred sixty dollars on his person which he requested be given to his attorney, Ben Laska. It would later prove to be part of the Urschel ransom.

Denver Police Chief Albert T. Clark and Captain Armstrong suspected that Bates had been involved in several past bank robberies in the Denver area. One was the twelve thousand dollar robbery of the National Bank at Louisville, Colorado, on January 20, 1932. Four witnesses positively identified him as the robber. Bates sent word to his wife, Clara, at their Pearl Street apartment through another prisoner being released. Mrs. Bates, aka Mrs. George Davis or Clara Feldman, paid the man two hundred dollars for the information, then sent a wire to Fort Worth detectives Weatherford and Swinney before leaving town:

*GEORGE L. DAVIS HELD IN DENVER WANTED IN BLUE RIDGE, TEXAS, BANK ROBBERY. WILL WAIVE*

*EXTRADITION. COME AT ONCE. ADVISE COMING BY
AIRPLANE.... GEORGE L. DAVIS*

When Swinney and Weatherford received the George
L. Davis wire, they remembered Kathryn's request
the night of the party. The Fort Worth detectives
turned the wire over to the FBI, who then took Bates
into custody, along with the money.

By mid-August 1933, just two weeks after the
release of Charles Urschel, the government was
preparing its case in Oklahoma City against
Kathryn's mother, Boss Shannon, Armon Shannon,
Bates, Bailey and the five money purchasers from St.
Paul. George and Kathryn could feel the net of the
law tightening, and panic began to set in. Enraged
that her mother was being held on a fifty thousand
dollar bond, on August 18, while in Des Moines,
Kathryn sent a note to the Oklahoma Assistant
Attorney General, Joseph B. Keenan, stating:

*The entire Urschel family and friends, and all of you
will be exterminated soon. There is no way I can
prevent it. I will gladly put George Kelly on the spot
for you if you will save my mother, who is innocent
of any wrongdoing. If you do not comply with this
request, there is no way in which I can prevent the
most awful tragedy. If you refuse my offer I shall
commit some minor offense and be placed in jail so
that you will know that I have no connection with the
terrible slaughter that will take place in Oklahoma
within the next few days.*

Kathryn then sent a telegram to her friend, Louise Magness, who was still staying at her Fort Worth home, asking her to fly to Des Moines. When Magness arrived she drove Kathryn and George to Brownwood, Texas, where, pretending to be George Kelly's sister, she purchased a 1928 Chevrolet sedan for them.

While incarcerated at the escape-proof Dallas County jail, Harvey Bailey, who had earned a reputation for his ability to escape from jails and prisons, bribed Deputy Sheriff Thomas L. Manion, and a jailer, Groover C. Bevill, to smuggle in a gun and two hacksaws to him. Two days and three hacksaws later, on Labor Day, September 4, after sawing through three bars allegedly with the help of the jailer, Bailey escaped from his cell, located on the tenth floor of the jail, around 7 o'clock in the morning, only to be captured the same day in Ardmore, Oklahoma, by a local police chief.

Both Manion and Bevill were indicted in Dallas, Texas, on September 25, and tried and convicted on October 5. Two days later, Manion was sentenced to pay a fine of ten thousand dollars and to serve two years in the United States Penitentiary at Leavenworth. Bevill was sentenced to serve fourteen months in the same institution. Years later, Bailey claimed the jailer brought the gun and saws in on his own with the plan to shoot Bailey and claim a reward.

With Bailey back in custody at the Oklahoma County jail in Oklahoma City, along with Bates, the elder Shannons and their son, Hoover notified Attorney General Cummings that he had ordered his agents to take complete control of the prisoners, even though they were in a county jail and not a federal facility. Hoover also ordered that no one be allowed to visit these prisoners, including their lawyers; and if a federal court ordered otherwise, the agents were to search any visiting attorney and an agent would be present at their interviews. No other prisoners were allowed in the jail, and Bailey, Bates, the Shannons, as well as their cells, were searched each day.

Bailey and Bates were restrained at all times in special handcuffs, and leg shackles that were chained to the floor. They were clothed only in undershorts and weren't allowed any reading or writing material. An armed FBI agent was stationed in front of their cells twenty-four hours a day; and on the first floor of the two-story jail, an FBI agent and a deputy sheriff guarded the entrance to the jail with machine guns. Three additional guards armed with machine guns were stationed across the street from the jail entrance, and the whole area was lighted by floodlights.

On the same day—Labor Day—that Bailey escaped from the Dallas County jail and was then recaptured, Kathryn picked up Luther Arnold, a part Indian itinerant, and his wife, Flossie Marie, and their twelve-year-old daughter, Geraldine, who were hitchhiking near Hillsboro, Texas. Out of work and destitute, the Depression refugees had only six dollars on them. Kathryn, driving a pickup truck and wearing a red wig, drove the Arnolds to Cleburne, Texas, and paid for their meals and lodging for the night. After revealing she was Kathryn Kelly, the following day she purchased clothes for Mrs. Arnold and her pre-teen, pimple-faced daughter and then gave Luther Arnold fifty dollars with instructions to go to Fort Worth, get in touch with her lawyer, and find out why Assistant Attorney General Keenan hadn't accepted her offer—that she would surrender Kelly and take a light sentence herself in exchange for the release of her mother, Ora Shannon. But the Government wasn't interested in a deal, and Luther returned to Cleburne to tell Kathryn.

Luther was then told to go to Oklahoma City and keep Kathryn informed of the trial. While in Oklahoma City, Luther picked up a letter at the General Delivery window of the post office which instructed him to go to 160 Mahncke Court in San Antonio where he was to meet Kathryn and his family. When he arrived, Kelly was also there, but left after spending one night.

Next, Kathryn got the Arnolds to agree to let Geraldine go with them on a short trip of 250 miles. Kathryn felt that Geraldine would provide a cover, making the Kellys look like a family of three while they travelled. She also gave Luther a letter to deliver to her father, James Emory Brooks, in

Oklahoma City, telling Brooks to give the bearer of the letter her pistol and any cash he could send.

Kathryn, George, and Geraldine then headed to Chicago, stopping on the way outside Coleman, Texas, to bury seventy-three thousand, two hundred fifty dollars of the ransom money on a farm owned by Kathryn's uncle, Cass Coleman. Later, Mrs. Arnold received a letter from Kathryn telling her that their trip had been extended and that she should join her husband in Oklahoma City to await the return of their daughter.

The offers of Bailey's attorney to negotiate and his request to have his client's trial moved to another state were refused by U.S. District Judge Edgar S. Vaught who had been assigned to the case, and on the morning of September 18, the largest, criminal trial of any kind in Southwest history got under way. The large number of perpetrators on trial were the first to be indicted and tried under the Lindbergh Kidnapping Law. Only George and Kathryn were missing from the defense table. Interestingly, the presiding judge also served as the administrator to the estate of Tom Slick, the late husband of Berenice Urschel.

On the next day, following the jury selection that provided for two alternates under the new federal law should one of the regular jurors become ill or otherwise incapacitated, Urschel received a threatening letter that was signed by Kelly:

*Just a few lines to let you know that I am getting my plans made to destroy your so-called mansion, and you and your family immediately after this trial. And young fellow, I guess you've begun to realize your serious mistake. Are you ignorant enough to think the Government can guard you forever. I gave you credit for more sense that that, and figured you thought too much of your family to jeopardize them as you have, but if you don't look out for them, why should we. I dislike hurting the innocent, but I told you exactly what would happen and you can bet $200,000 more everything I said will be true. You are living on borrowed time now. You know that the Shannon family are victims of circumstances the same as you was. You don't seem to mind prosecuting the innocent, neither will I have conscious qualms over brutally murdering your family. The Shannons have put the heat on, but I don't desire to see them prosecuted as they are innocent and I have a much better method of settling with them. As far as the guilty being punished you would probably have lived the rest of your life in peace had you tried only the guilty, but if the Shannons are convicted look out, and God help you for he is the only one that will be able to do you any good. In the event of my arrest I've already formed an outfit to take care of and destroy you and yours the same as if I was there. I am spending your money to have you and your family killed – nice – eh? You are bucking people who have cash – planes, bombs and unlimited connection both here and* *abroad. I have friends in Oklahoma City that know every move and every plan you make, and you are still too dumb to figure out the finger man there. If my brain was no larger than yours, the Government would have had me long ago, as it is I am drinking good beer and will yet see you and your family like I should have left you at first – stone dead. I don't worry about Bates and Bailey. They will be out for the ceremonies – your slaughter. Now I say – it is up to you; if the Shannons are convicted, you can get another rich wife in hell, because that will be the only place you can use one. Adios, smart one. Your worst enemy, GEO. R. KELLY I will put my fingerprints below so you can't say some crank wrote this.*

Urschel and his family responded:

*We are eager for this letter to be published so the people of the United States will know it is no fabrication from the air and will know the sort of people we have defied and are opposed to. We still have faith in the ultimate success of the federal government in its struggle with crime, and are gambling the safety of every member of our group on that success…. The Urschel family does not waste one moment in giving gangland its answer.*

To reinforce his point, Urschel sat prominently in the front row of the courtroom throughout the trial.

Angered by Kelly's letter, Special Assistant Keenan also responded:

*We appreciate fully the patriotic response of Mr. Urschel in casting aside personal considerations. It is encouraging to the government in its drive to wipe out gangster depredations. The federal government will respond by giving Mr. Urschel and his family full protection. Neither Mr. Urschel nor anyone else will be left to further attacks of the underworld.*

Even though Kelly's fingerprints were smudged all over the letter, it was believed that Kathryn had been responsible for it, prompting E.E. Kirkpatrick to call Kathryn a "Human Tigress" fifteen years later when she unsuccessfully applied for parole. J. Edgar Hoover himself referred to her in his book *Persons in Hiding* (widely known to have been ghostwritten by his publicist, Courtney Ryley Cooper) as "a woman of superior intelligence" and "one of the most coldly deliberate criminals of my experience." George Machine Gun Kelly was also gaining notoriety when a local police officer called him "one of the most vicious and dangerous criminals in America."

Judge Vaught and prosecuting attorney Herbert K. Hyde also received threatening letters either from George or Kathryn, which were followed by a rambling hand-written letter addressed "For Editor" at the *Daily Oklahoman,* proclaiming the innocence of the Shannon family. The newspaper published it in its entirety on page one on September 20. Judge Vaught and Herbert Hyde were assigned body guards by the FBI.

# CHAPTER 7

## In Hiding

The Kellys were not welcome in Chicago. They were put up for a while by Abe and Charles Caplan, owners of a Michigan Avenue tavern. Joe Bergl, a former friend of Kelly's and Cicero garage owner, didn't want to have anything to do with them, but he did provide them with a Chevrolet car, two hundred dollars, and a quart of whiskey so they would leave his place.

On September 21, Kathryn and George left Chicago taking the Arnolds' daughter, Geraldine, with them. The day after their departure from the Windy City, members of the Barker-Karpis Gang drove a bulletproof Hudson automobile, equipped with smoke screen and oil slick devices, in the robbery of a

Federal Reserve Bank messenger. During the escape, the bandits wrecked the car and killed a Chicago police officer. The car was traced back to Joe Bergl. Inside the car were several license plates from different states. One set of 1933 Illinois plates (699-493) was issued to J.J. Rosenburg, of 3818 West Roosevelt Road, Chicago. J.J. Rosenburg was an alias of George Kelly's, thus making him one of the prime suspects along with Verne Miller who was recently rumored to be in Chicago. The authorities theorized that the two men were attempting to raise cash to spring Harvey Bailey. "Pretty Boy" Floyd, Adam Richetti, and Clifford "Kip" Harback would also be named as suspects.

Nearly a month earlier, a gang of machine gunners had staged a similar raid in St. Paul when messengers from the Stockyards National Bank were robbed on the steps of South St. Paul post office of thirty-three thousand dollars. One policeman was killed and another wounded. Police theorized that both robberies were the work of the same gang, the "Southwestern gang of Verne Miller and Machine Gun Kelly."

Newspapers erroneously reported that ballistics tests proved the guns used in both the Chicago and St. Paul killings were the same guns used in the Kansas City Massacre. In fact, a machine gun stolen from the murdered St. Paul officer would be recovered by the FBI from Arthur "Doc" Barker's Chicago apartment after his arrest in January 1935, thereby connecting both the St. Paul and Chicago crimes to the Barker-Karpis gang.

Desperate for a place to hide, the Kellys headed for Memphis, Tennessee, the place of George's boyhood home and where he had attended school. At the same time, Kathryn's Shannon relatives, Albert Bates, Harvey Bailey, along with Edward Berman and Clifford Skelly, the two money-changers, were on trial in Oklahoma City before Federal District Judge Edgar S. Vaught convicted of conspiracy to violate the new federal kidnapping law. The "Lindbergh Law," as it was called, had been introduced after the abduction and murder of Charles Augustus Lindbergh, Jr., the son of well-known aviator Charles Lindbergh and Anne Morrow Lindbergh, a year earlier, and it allowed the FBI to become involved in cases where state lines had been crossed or, in the absence of evidence to the contrary, when it was presumed the boundaries had been violated. The law also provided penalties of life in prison.

The kidnapping of Charles Urschel, the capture of Bailey and Bates, and the nationwide search under way for Machine Gun Kelly and his wife Kathryn had attracted national attention. Reporters poured into Oklahoma City from all over the country to cover the trial. Heavy security surrounded the defendants, the jury, the judge, Assistant Attorney General Joseph Keenan (who had been sent by Attorney General Cummings to manage the prosecution's case), and the local U.S. attorney, creating an atmosphere of suspense that was enhanced further by rumors that associates of Bates and Bailey had arrived in Oklahoma City with plans to liberate them.

It is interesting to note that Bruce Barnes, in his biography of his father, claims that when the Kellys left the Shannon ranch after releasing Urschel, they drove immediately to Cass Coleman's farm and buried most of George's share of the money, partly in a vacuum jug and the balance in a molasses can. They chose a spot near a mesquite tree in a cotton patch, then raked the ground around the entire area to conceal any tell-tale footprints they might have left. Kathryn started wearing a red wig, and George bleached his hair blond. "Over the next several weeks, George would gain twenty pounds to further alter his image.

The two drove to Juarez, Mexico, passing through Midland and El Paso, Texas, along the way. They left Juarez on August 3 and spent the day driving to Chihuahua, where they checked into Hotel Palacio, the city's leading hotel. They registered as Mr. and Mrs. George Ramsey Kelly of Dallas, Texas." Convinced they had pulled off the perfect kidnapping, they spent the next several days relaxing and exploring the surrounding area.

On the afternoon of August 12, as they were resting in their hotel room and listening to the radio, the regular program was interrupted with the announcement that the Shannon ranch had been raided, and that Kathryn's family had been arrested.

The news report also said that Albert Bates was arrested in Denver, and four other men caught with the ransom money had been taken into custody in St. Paul. Bruce Barnes claims that his father "spoke fluent Spanish," which was why he could understand the news broadcast. After hearing the broadcast, the Kellys then headed back to El Paso where they stored their automobile—a two-toned black and blue 1932 sixteen-cylinder Cadillac coupe, and flew first to Denver, Colorado, then to Des Moines, Iowa, eventually ending up in Memphis.

It was during this time that Kathryn passed word through a Fort Worth attorney named Sam Sayers that in return for leniency for herself and her mother, she would be willing to surrender her infamous husband. Documents, now on file at a National Archives warehouse in Fort Worth, show an undated telegram from the U.S. Attorney's office in Fort Worth to U.S. Attorney Herbert K. Hyde of Oklahoma City, reporting an offer by Sayers' law firm to surrender Kelly in return for leniency for Kathryn and her mother.

By September 7, Hyde had passed the offer on to Joseph B. Keenan, the special assistant attorney general who had been charged with heading the government's war against gangsters and racketeers. In a letter to Hyde, Keenan flatly rejected any deal which would deprive the government of the right to deal with Kelly, Bates, and Bailey as it saw fit, including seeking the death penalty under the new kidnapping law. However, Keenan added that if the government could get Kelly and the ransom money, "I am hoping that Judge (Edgar S.) Vaught could see his way clear to being very lenient to Mrs. Shannon and Mrs. Kelly, even to the point of absolute release... if we had a free hand to deal with Kelly, Bates, and Bailey as the facts justify."

Luther, who had been picked up by the FBI in Oklahoma City when he had traveled there to pay one of the Kellys' lawyers, confirmed that Kelly seemed to be willing to go along with the deal. Arnold told the agents that he had overheard Kathryn and George discussing the matter, and that Kelly had told Kathryn, "Well go ahead and make your dicker and when you get it made, let me know. I'm willing to go, but you know I can't go to them and do any dickering." For some reason, the deal was never made.

# CHAPTER 8

## The First Trial

**W**ith Charles Urschel's courage and remarkable memory now on display from the witness stand in the proceedings against Bates and the three Shannons, seven other defendants, apprehended for trying to exchange the ransom money they had purchased, were awaiting their appearance before Judge Vaught. In light of the threatening letters received from the Kellys, security in and around the courthouse remained tight with every available officer on duty openly carrying machine guns, sawed-off shotguns, and revolvers. The body guards of Judge Vaught and the prosecuting attorney were on high alert. Inside the courthouse, all elevators were blocked off two levels below the ninth-floor courtroom. Everyone was required to be patted down and the contents of women's pocketbooks inspected before walking up the two flights of stairs to the courtroom itself, also heavily guarded by armed deputies.

Inside the courtroom it was standing room only. With temperatures reaching 90 degrees and no air conditioning, most of the spectators used either a newspaper or palm leaf fan to stir the air. Many of the attendees were women from the city's upper level of society who had brought lunch so they wouldn't lose their seats by leaving. Coats and ties were required for men, although an exception was made for the jurors. The ladies dressed fashionably.

Berenice Urschel and the Jarretts were the first to take the stand, testifying briefly. Next, it was Charles Urschel's turn.  Dressed in his customary dark business suit, he told the court all that he remembered. He later positively identified the Shannons. In addition, he identified George Kelly's machine gun (Government's Exhibit No. 9), the chain that had been used to restrain him, the dipper he had drunk well water from with the broken-off handle. Other testimony included the ransom correspondence sent to his family and photographs of Armon's shack. When he was shown Government's Exhibit No. 8, a photo, he positively identified George Kelly: "He is the other man." The three hundred or so spectators and jurors would remain spellbound as Urschel talked about the conversations that had taken place between him and

Kelly, and that Kelly seemed to know a great deal about automobiles, especially the mechanics.

The trial continued for the better part of twelve days, during which time there was a suspected attempt to kidnap or possibly kill the head county jailer or his wife and children. The jailer, his family, and their house were placed under heavy guard.

Also about this time, Oklahoma rancher and frontier lawman Charles Francis Colcord, who was a close friend of Urschel's, called a meeting at the Colcord Building of the richest men in Oklahoma City and put together a fifteen thousand dollar reward for information leading to the capture and conviction of Machine Gun Kelly and Kathryn, dead or alive. Colcord, who had been Oklahoma City's first chief of police forty-three years earlier, told a *Daily Oklahoman* interviewer:

*An outraged citizenship feels that something should be done to assist our federal and state governments in stamping out crime in this country, and particularly kidnapping…. I am offering a reward of $10,000 in cash for the delivery of George Francis "Machine Gun" Kelly, charged with the kidnapping of Charles F. Urschel, to the sheriff of Oklahoma County, or to any agent or officer of the U.S. Department of Justice; and a reward of $5,000 in cash for the delivery of Kathryn Kelly, wife of George Francis Kelly, charged as a conspirator in the kidnapping of Charles F. Urschel, to the sheriff of Oklahoma County, or to any agent or officer of the*

*U.S. Department of Justice. If, in the making of the captures or arrests, either of said parties should be killed, the respective reward will be paid.*

# PHOTOS

James Brooks and Ora with daughter, Cleo (Kathryn)

Kathryn

Kathryn before she met Machine Gun Kelly

The Barnes Home

Thompson Machine Gun - gift from Kathryn to George

Machine Gun Kelly's mugshot

George "Machine Gun" Kelly and Kathryn Kelly in 1933

Kathryn and George in happier times

Kathryn captured in Memphis-1933

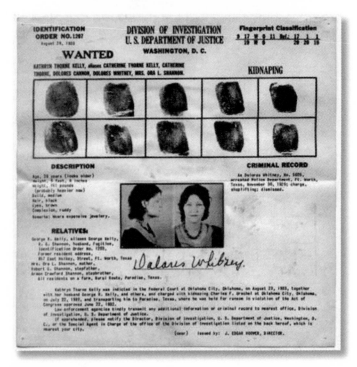

Kathryn's FBI ID card with the name Delores Whitney

Agent Rorer (left) and Kathryn Kelly

Kathryn slaps guard

Kathryn awaiting trial

Ora and Kathryn leave court

Kathryn and George in court

Photo of letter sent by Kathryn and George

Geraldine testifies

Bates, Bailey, Armon, and Ora Shannon
during sentencing

Milan Prison

George "Machine Gun" Kelly in jail

Kathryn and Ora finally released from prison

J. Edgar Hoover

Urschel mansion

Charles Urschel

Shannon farmhouse where Urschel was held

Geneva Ramsey

The Coleman Sisters
(*back row* -Inez and Ora - *front row*- Ima and Pearl)

"Machine Gun" Kelly's hideout
at 1408 Rayner St, Memphis, Tennessee

Pauline and Ora

Ora working as clerk in store

Kellys' hideout at Mulkey address

Cemetery where "Machine
Gun" Kelly
is buried

George Kelly's
headstone

# CHAPTER 9

## The Arrest

The Kellys, with Geraldine Arnold still with them, arrived in Memphis, the town that George was all too familiar with and where his ex-wife continued to live. Not knowing where to go, Kelly first tried to contact George Ramsey, Jr.., his brother-in-law from his first marriage to Geneva, but he was out of town. He then contacted Langford Ramsey, the younger brother of George Ramsey, Jr., and told him that he and Kathryn needed a place to stay.

Ramsey, who had recently passed the Tennessee bar exam, directed them to the home of some friends where they could rent a room for twenty-five dollars a week, the same place Kelly had stayed earlier before Kathryn joined him. Owned by John Tichenor, a used-car salesman, and his brother-in-law, Seymour Travis, a grocery clerk, Tichenor lived in the house with his wife and kids, who were out of town.

It was at this house, 1408 Rayner, a quiet street off South Parkway, that George asked Langford to set up a meeting at Langford's house on Mignon with his two sons by his first marriage. By then Geneva had already remarried, and she and her husband, Frank Trimbach, recently promoted to national advertising manager for Rexall Drug Company, were in the process of moving the family from St. Louis to Boston where the corporate headquarters was located. Kelly's sons didn't know who he was and at Kelly's request, he was introduced to them as an old family friend. He gave them each a twenty dollar bill and told them he was a federal agent, and he'd been on a special mission. That's why he hadn't been around.

The Kellys had about run out of money. In an act of desperation, Kelly gave Ramsey his Chevrolet and sent him to retrieve Kathryn's furs as well as some of the money they had left behind, buried in Thermos jugs and molasses tins at Cass Coleman's farm in Texas. Kelly had Geraldine go with him as a guide to show him the way.

When the two arrived, Coleman informed Ramsey that the FBI was watching the place and refused to give him Kathryn's furs—a Japanese mink coat, a black lamb coat, and a silver fox coat, which he had stuffed in a trash bag inside a large bucket and hidden in the oats in the barn, or let him dig up the money. Ramsey wired Kelly telling him that "the deal fell through." He then put Geraldine on a train to Oklahoma City and wired Luther Arnold that his daughter was coming home.

Unknown to Ramsey, the Arnolds had already been arrested and the FBI intercepted Ramsey's wire. Geraldine was met at the station by her father, who immediately took her to meet with federal officer Ralph Colvin. She was able to tell them everything that Kathryn and Machine Gun Kelly had done since she had been traveling with them. She also told them that they were staying in Memphis with a man named "Tich." A Memphis police officer checked the telephone directory and found a listing for John Tichenor, a motor car dealer. Thinking that this might be "Tich," they put his house under round-the-clock surveillance. After a couple of days, they were convinced that the Kellys were inside. With the information supplied by twelve-year-old Geraldine Arnold, the Memphis police and the FBI set out to arrest the Kellys on the morning of September 26, 1933, at the Tichenor home.

There are several versions of how the arrest of George and Kathryn Kelly took place. One story suggests that George had stepped outside to retrieve the morning paper and unintentionally left the front door unlocked. The feds and city detectives, posing as garbage workers, sneaked into the house and immediately subdued George in the bathroom and Kathryn who was in the process of dressing in the bedroom. It was then, according to folklore and rumor, that George yelled, "Don't shoot, G-men," thus coining the nickname G-Men for the government federal agents headed up by J. Edgar Hoover. Kelly would later deny ever using the term "G-man" and, in fact, some reports claim that Kathryn herself was the first to use the term when once captured, she put her arm around George and said, "These G-men are never going to leave us alone."

Another version states that just before dawn, a dozen men armed with shotguns and machine guns crept up to the small brick house in South Memphis, kicked in the front door, and burst inside. Cowering in a corner of the living room was an unarmed George Kelly, who immediately raised his arms and cried, "Don't shoot, G-men. Don't shoot." He had apparently put his pistol down on a sewing machine next to where he was standing.

Newspapers reported that Sergeant William Raney of the Memphis Police Department knocked on the door of the Tichenor home. When Kelly opened the door and stuck out his .45 automatic, a weapon Kelly had gotten Travis to purchase for him, Raney pushed his shotgun against Kelly's stomach, bringing about Kelly's surrender.

There is also the story, widely circulated by the FBI Director Hoover at the time, that Kelly, when realizing he couldn't escape, groveled and cried, "Don't shoot, G-men." Regardless, the term "G-men", which had applied to all federal investigators, entered into the vernacular of the English language as a reference to FBI agents.

Writer and historian Rick Mattix reports that "Sergeant Raney, armed with a sawed-off shotgun, entered Kelly's bedroom where he found him in his pajamas, hung over, and holding a .45. Kathryn was asleep on the bed." During the night, the couple had apparently consumed six quarts of gin. The sergeant jammed his shotgun into Kelly's stomach and ordered him to drop the gun, which Kelly did, on his own foot. "I have been waiting for you all night," Kelly was said to have muttered.

A more humorous version comes from Kelly's son, Bruce Barnes, who claims that Tichenor told him that Kelly had picked up the morning newspaper but failed to re-lock the front door. He walked into the bathroom and while there the police entered the house. When the police burst into the bathroom, Kelly was still relieving himself. Although his gun was in the bathroom, he didn't have time to grab it.

*The Memphis Flyer* provides a more detailed description. On the night of September 25, 1933, Kelly stayed awake by reading a *Master Detective* magazine. He was halfway through "My Blood-Curdling Ride with Death" when a soft thump outside startled him. Peeking through the windows, he saw the noise was only the newspaper tossed onto the porch by the paper boy. Kelly stepped outside in his underwear and picked up the paper. When he went back inside, he walked down the hallway to the bathroom, forgetting to lock the door behind him. At that moment, two cars pulled up outside the house. Sergeant William J. Raney, along with other detectives from the Memphis Police Department and special agents from the FBI, approached the front door. To his surprise, it was unlocked. Sawed-off shotgun at the ready, the detective stepped into the living room and found it unoccupied. Through an open doorway Raney could glimpse Tichenor and Travis asleep in a front bedroom as he moved down the hallway. Just then Kelly stepped out of the bathroom, the pistol in his hand. Seeing the shotgun aimed at his heart, he surrendered. "Okay, boys," he said, nearly shooting himself in the foot when he dropped his gun to the floor. "I've been waiting all night for you." To which the officer replied, "Well, here we are." The other seven men who had entered the house found Kathryn asleep in a back room. She screamed as George put on his own handcuffs and refused to put her street clothes on. But the fifty-six day run beginning in Paradise, Texas, and ending in Memphis, Tennessee, was over. The government's Public Enemy Number One had been apprehended. A quick search of the premises and Kelly's Chevrolet turned up empty beer and gin bottles and ashtrays overflowing with cigarette butts, but no ransom bills or anything of value.

The Kellys were taken into custody, along with John Tichenor and his brother-in-law, Seymore E. Travis, by FBI agents and Memphis police. On the same day, George and Kathryn were arraigned at the Shelby County jail in Memphis where they both pled not guilty to kidnapping Charles Urschel, and bond was set at one hundred thousand dollars each.

Kathryn faked an appendicitis attack, which required a medical examination from a doctor, and attempted to bribe one of the jailers, offering him fifteen thousand dollars to let her out. When that didn't work, she then waived extradition, stating that her family had been coerced into helping with the kidnapping, which consisted of watching over and feeding Urschel. This was the same story the three Shannon family members were telling during their trial that was taking place in Oklahoma City, claiming that they were in fear of Kelly.

Kathryn told the authorities that she had wanted to surrender and testify on her family's behalf, but her husband threatened to kill her. "I am glad we are both arrested," Kathryn told the Memphis police chief, "because I am not guilty and I can prove it. I'll be rid of him and that bunch. I don't want to say anything about that guy Kelly, but he got me into this terrible mess and I don't want to have anything more to do with him."

Kelly, on the other hand, declared he would fight extradition to Oklahoma, and when placed in a cell, he said, "I'll be out of this in no time. Let's see them keep me."

At a news conference that morning following the arrest and arraignment, Chief of Police Will D. Lee gave reporters the details of the capture with his own flourishes:

*When Kelly looked into the muzzle of a sawed-off shotgun in the hands of a Memphis detective sergeant, there was a thin yellow fluid that began to rise up the canal of his spinal column, in much the fashion that mercury rises in a thermometer on an exceedingly hot day, and he immediately dropped his revolver and submitted quietly to arrest.*

Detective Raney added to Lee's remarks with a few of his own boasts.

*Kelly was never nearer death than he was at that time. If he had raised one finger I would have blown him in two. When I shoved my gun into his stomach, he dropped his .45 as meekly as a lamb.*

That afternoon the banner headline published by the *Press-Scimitar* read:

*MACHINE GUN KELLY CAPTURED IN MEMPHIS*

On September 26, the International News Service reported:

*George "Machine Gun" Kelly, America's no. 1 desperado, sought for a series of abductions, bank holdups and massacres that have terrorized the nation, fell into the clutches of the law today. The man who had sent the organized forces of law of the 48 states and the federal government on the greatest manhunt in history, taunting his pursuers with scornful, threatening letters, surrendered meekly to Department of Justice agents who trapped him in a Memphis hideout.*

When Urschel learned of the Kellys' capture, he shuttered the company offices and told his employees they were free to attend the trial or just relax on their own for a few days.

Ironically, as Kathryn and Machine Gun Kelly were being arrested, ten inmates, including all of the members of the future Dillinger gang, escaped from the penitentiary in Michigan City, Indiana.

Following the arrest, the newspaper reports were still pointing out that Kelly was wanted for participating in the Kansas City Massacre, as well as the murder of a policeman in St. Paul, and the killing of the police officer in Chicago. The Chicago Chief of Detectives William "Shoes" Schoemaker asked government officials to extradite Kelly to stand trial in Chicago before taking him to Oklahoma City. When Kelly learned of this, the following day he told FBI Agent W.A. Rorer, "You've got me right on the Urschel kidnapping, but not the Chicago robbery or the Kansas City Union Station job." Kelly agreed to waive extradition and return to Oklahoma City.

# CHAPTER 10

## The First Trial Concludes

**K**athryn's campaign to create an image of her husband as one of the most famous and ruthless criminals in America had worked. With the trial of the original defendants—Harvey Bailey, Albert Bates, Robert and Ora Shannon, Armon Shannon, and the two money-changes, Edward Berman and Clifford Skelly—still taking place in Oklahoma City, it was decided to keep the Kellys in Memphis until it was time for them to testify for fear that their presence at the trial might intimidate potential witnesses.

Newspapers, such as *The Commercial Appeal,* played up this fear as well: "Kelly is a ruthless killer in any light in which he is viewed. If he has ever shown the slightest degree of mercy for the victims of his criminal records, it is not on record." However, Charles Urschel disputed this claim when he testified that he was treated "with consideration" before being released unharmed. And Kelly, though confessing to the kidnapping charge, strongly denied taking part in any murders. Ballistics tests proved he was telling the truth, eventually linking the Chicago policeman's murder and the Kansas City "massacre" to others. By way of an exclamation point, in *The Encyclopedia of American Crime,* author Carl Sifakis notes: "The fact is that Kelly never fired a shot at anyone and he certainly never killed anyone, a remarkable statistic for a public enemy dubbed 'Machine Gun.'"

For a while, both Kathryn and George seemed to enjoy their notoriety.  Kelly even joked with his guards—"Say, lend me that machine gun for just a minute, will you?" and complained about the accommodations—"This cell's not big enough to swing a cat in. But that doesn't matter; I won't be in here long." Likewise, Kathryn cheerfully smiled and posed for newsreel cameramen from Fox, Paramount, and other agencies who had flown to Memphis just for a glimpse of the fugitives. Even in her prison garb, she was photogenic.

Within days, though, Kathryn grew tired of the incessant questioning, telling reporters she was just an innocent victim. Kelly was equally tired of numerous photo sessions and angry over the fact that he had to wear leg shackles: "What do they have to put these things on for? Do you think I'm going anywhere, with these guards watching me and these bars?"

It didn't matter; Memphis authorities weren't taking any chances. Elaborate security precautions were put into place. Kelly was moved to the top floor of the jail where he was the sole prisoner, watched around the clock by machine-gun-toting guards. Because there was fear of a gangland reprisal—someone shooting Kelly to keep him from testifying—no reporters or visitors were allowed near him.

In the meantime, FBI agents visited the Coleman farm, arrested Kathryn's uncle, Cass Coleman, and dug up the buried money—seventy-three thousand, two hundred fifty dollars. Later, Albert Bates' wife, Clara Feldman, would tell agents where she had hidden another thirty-six thousand, three hundred forty dollars of the ransom. Clara's brother-in-law, Alvin H. Scott, would be caught with thirteen hundred sixty dollars in Urschel money after an auto accident at Rosenburg, Oregon, and would disclose the location of another sixty-one hundred forty dollars.

Meanwhile, the trial in Oklahoma City continued, with Charles Urschel finishing on the witness stand, followed by testimony from the elder Shannons and their son Armon. Bates, having already been identified by Urschel, had no defense and, therefore, didn't take the stand. The constantly tobacco-chewing Bailey also declined to testify, even though the only evidence against him was the ransom money that had been found in his pocket.

In concluding the trial of the original defendants in the Urschel kidnapping case, Keenan, the U.S. prosecutor from Washington, addressed the jurors dramatically:

*If this government cannot protect its citizens, then we had better... turn it over to the Kellys and the Bateses, the Baileys and the others of the underworld and pay tribute to them through taxes. Kidnapping has become a modern art. The plotters lay their vicious plans, bold strong-armed men carry out the abduction, hirelings stand guard, and later, when ransom has been paid, the money-changers arrange for its dissemination through underworld channels. In this case the government has shown you the whole picture of how this heinous scheme was conceived and carried out.*

*Through four states of the Union these criminals plied their trade and defied the government. A single state could not control such swift operations. The federal government was forced to step in and take a hand. Now that government has been defied by these gangsters and we have caught them red-handed, we are convinced that they are all guilty of this conspiracy and demand that a verdict of guilty be returned.*

District Attorney Herbert K. Hyde then presented his final argument:

*I beg of you, in the name of my government, to return a verdict of guilty against these defendants. This is one of the most important cases ever tried. Precedents are being set that will guide the courts and the bar in all future trials that grow out of this determined effort of your government to stamp out this most damnable of crimes—kidnapping.*

The jurors, who had been sequestered throughout the trial, were served a final supper of chicken-fried steak and mashed potatoes and gravy. Then they took but a single ballot to find Bates, Bailey, the three Shannons, and the two money changers guilty as charged—the sealed verdicts to be read in court first thing the following morning. It had taken the jury less than two hours to decide the fate of the defendants. On September 30, George and Kathryn's third wedding anniversary, seven of the accused were found guilty of participating in the Urschel kidnapping. Judge Edgar S. Vaught read the jury's verdict:

The defendants, Albert L. Bates, Harvey J. Bailey, R.G. Shannon, Ora L. Shannon, Armon Crawford Shannon, Edward Berman, and Clifford Skelly will please stand. Now, in this case, the jury has returned the verdict of guilty. The court is of the opinion that this verdict is fully sustained by the evidence.

Three others—Isadore "Kid Cann Blumenfeld, Sam Kronick and Sam Kozbert—were acquitted.

It was the decision of the court to delay sentencing until after George and Kathryn entered their pleas of "guilty." Sentences were to be announced the following week.

On October 1, the Kellys were flown to Oklahoma City on a chartered American Airways amid a convoy of nine airplanes. When they arrived, Kelly spoke to a group of photographers, "Hello, gang, nice trip." Not wanting a repeat of the massacre that took place in Kansas City, one of the guards held a machine gun on Kelly, while another officer kept one trained on the crowd. Prosecutor Hyde, who arrived with Mr. and Mrs. Urschel, were also at the airport. "That's the man," Urschel exclaimed when he saw Kelly. From inside the car, Mrs. Urschel stated, "That face will haunt me for as long as I live." The Kellys were then rushed to a motorcade of ten automobiles and taken to the county jail.

Kathryn had been expected to testify on behalf of her family, but she never took the stand. A newspaper erroneously reported that both Kellys were going to plead guilty and stand with the other convicted participants from the first trial to receive their sentences. However, the Kellys surprised everyone when on October 7, just prior to Federal Judge Edward S. Vaught handing down sentences on the original defendants, they entered a plea of not guilty, thereby requiring that there be another trial. Judge Vaught had no choice but to continue with the sentencing of the other seven defendants.

Bates, Bailey, and Kathryn's mother and stepfather, Ora and R.G. Shannon, were sentenced to life, while the Shannons' twenty-two-year-old son, Armon Shannon, received ten years' probation. The court felt that he had only acted as a loyal son, and wasn't mentally capable of contributing to the kidnapping itself. Therefore, he was allowed to return to Paradise to his wife and two children, one of them a week-old son he hadn't even seen. Edward Berman and Clifford Skelly, who had been money-changers in the crime, were each sentenced to five years.

Ora and Boss were stunned. Kathryn was reported to have stared at the judge icily as she listened to Judge Vaught sentence her mother to life in prison. Then she broke down. Following the sentencing, Kelly passed Urschel on his way from the court room. "You'll get yours yet, you _____," he threatened, drawing his index finger across his jugular vein.

The following day, Bates and Bailey were taken to Leavenworth to begin their sentences. Boss Shannon was allowed sixty days to get his business affairs in order. Ora Shannon was granted ten days to dispose of her property. At some point during those ten days, Kathryn sent Ora a letter telling her not to get rid of "Sweet Sixteen," her sixteen cylinder Cadillac, because she would have a need for it "very soon." Kathryn was either convinced she would be acquitted, or she was still planning to escape. It had been revealed by the US Attorney from Amarillo, Texas, that the Kellys had passports to Germany.

# CHAPTER 11

## The Second Trial

The separate trial for George and Kathryn began on October 9, and Judge Vaught again was on the bench. As in the first trial, he had turned down all pleas for delays or change of venue. With a conviction being a foregone conclusion, the courtroom was only half full, and security not as tight.

When the Kellys arrived at the courthouse the first morning, Kathryn saw her father standing near the elevator. As she paused to kiss his cheek, federal agent J.C. White shoved her, hard enough that she fell against another agent and lost a heel off her shoe. When he did, Kathryn turned around and slapped him. George then tried to strike the agent with his manacled hands only to be pistol whipped on one side of his face and in the back of his head. Kathryn screamed, "Don't! Don't!" but was later seen chatting with the agent as if nothing had taken place.

Kelly entered the courtroom with swelling on his left temple holding a bloody handkerchief up to his face. The night before the trial was to begin, he had stomped on the shallow plate holding his meager dinner rations. He had been on bread and water since his threatening gesture to Urschel.

On the first day of the trial, not only was a complete twelve-man jury selected—a carpenter, three utility company workers, a filling station operator, a general store owner, a grocer, and five farmers, but the government called nearly half of their witnesses. Judge Vaught seemed determined to move the case to a conclusion as quickly as possible. The day before he had received an anonymous threatening letter: "If you do not dismiss these people, you and your family will be killed and your house will be blown up." He was not intimidated. "Men such as Kelly, who write letters boasting what they are going to do, seldom carry out their threats. As a federal judge, I could hardly be expected to show the white feather to hoodlums."

Keenan, who had also received threats, made his own statement: "We are ready to meet the challenge of these gangsters and outlaws fearlessly and with their own weapons. The government intends to stamp out these outrages if it takes the United

States Army to do it, but that will not be necessary. This statement is made in deadly earnest and with no desire to be melodramatic."

Director Hoover added his statements as well, published in an interview with United News Service:

*Kelly's capture means something to the underworld that the average person doesn't understand. The criminal fears death more than anything else. At heart they are all rats—dirty yellow rats. A gangster will kill you, oh sure, if he has a machine gun and you are absolutely helpless. They like to think they are above the law. But they actually operate most of the time with one eye on the electric chair. The underworld doesn't like to feel that our men or the police can reach in with a moment's notice and pluck their big shots out of bed—and that's just what we have been doing.*

The evidence was overwhelming against the Kellys. Mr. and Mrs. Urschel testified, along with John Catlett who received the ransom notes. The testimony that followed focused on Kathryn's involvement in the kidnapping, which up until that time had still been in question.

Luther William Arnold, the unemployed worker with a potential government charge hanging over his head for his involvement, took the stand and testified that after Kathryn picked them up, she identified herself and talked about all of the problems the Shannon family was going through because of Charles Urschel. Arnold told the court, "Mrs. Kelly said they ought to have killed the son of a bitch and that she wished she could do it herself."

Mrs. Arnold testified how their twelve-year-old daughter Geraldine had virtually been kidnapped by a red-haired woman in a blue gingham dress who drove a Model-A Ford light truck. The woman identified herself as Kathryn Kelly. "I let her have my baby for a little ride," she claimed. "She said she would be back that day. It was two weeks before I saw her again."

Geraldine's own testimony was equally damaging when she told the jury about her ordeal and said that Kelly threatened to kill Judge Vaught, Charles Urschel, and the prosecutors who were handling the case against the Shannons. When the trial was over, Geraldine collected four thousand dollars of the fifteen thousand dollar reward that had been offered for the Kellys, but not without some legal contention. A citizens committee, composed of Charles Urschel and his business associates, that had been appointed presumably to advise Colcord on the proper distribution of the reward, issued a statement saying: "... no part of the reward will be paid to anyone, investigation having shown that the federal agents who captured the Kellys were acting on information which they had in their possession before the reward was offered. The agents themselves are not permitted by the government to accept rewards."

As far as the Arnolds themselves, it was Urschel's belief that their assistance was obtained only in return for not sending them to the penitentiary with the others, and, in fact, it had been determined from Boss Shannon's statements to Special Agent in Charge F.J. Blake that they were old friends of Kathryn. She had known Luther Arnold and his wife eleven years—ever since Geraldine was one year old. The story that Kathryn had picked up the Arnolds on the road was a fabrication. She had gone to the Arnolds' home to see them and got them to agree to go with her as a blind. For their assistance, Kathryn paid Arnold sixteen hundred dollars.

Even with these statements, attorneys Jack Burroughs and P.D. Smith in representing Geraldine prepared to file a lawsuit on behalf of their young client, naming Colcord and other members of the reward committee as defendants. Before the filing could take place, however, and not wanting to risk any negative press or adverse criticism, it was agreed that Geraldine should receive a portion of the original reward—four thousand dollars—and payment was made by Judge Lucius Babock.

The FBI agent who had questioned the Kellys in Memphis offered another twist to the discussion of Urschel's possible fate, testifying that Kelly told him he'd met with Verne Miller, who was wanted for several murders and for allegedly being one of the killers at the Union Station Massacre. "He [Kelly] and Verne Miller had agreed that one or the other would kill Mr. Urschel," the agent testified. He also testified that they agreed to kill Mr. Jarrett as well.

Ralph Colvin, the special agent in the FBIs Oklahoma City office, was the next to testify, stating that Kathryn said that Mr. Urschel didn't have long to live if he won the suit to seize certain jewelry from her that had been located in a safe deposit box in Fort Worth. "She said she couldn't afford to lose that jewelry because it was all she had left to provide for her daughter, Pauline...."

When Agent Colvin finished testifying, eighteen-year-old Gay Coleman, Kathryn's cousin, related how George had mentioned during the midday dinner in early July, "There's more'n apt to be a kidnapping in Oklahoma City soon." And that Kathryn had bragged, "We're going to be in the big money before long."

Cass Coleman, Kathryn's uncle, told the jury about the couple's short stay there while attempting to escape the law, and that his niece had several loud verbal exchanges with Kelly regarding the hiding of the ransom money claiming that Kathryn referred to Kelly as "that damned fool."

Another witness was Kathryn's stepsister, twelve-year-old Ruth Shannon. She recounted how Kathryn had appeared unannounced early Sunday—the day Urschel was in transit from Oklahoma City to Paradise—and took her along with Armon's young pregnant wife and baby, and Kathryn's daughter Pauline to Kathryn's Fort Worth home where they all stayed for ten days. Kathryn had told them it was just so the four of them could do some window-shopping, see a few moving pictures shows, and have some fun in the big city, and also visit Kathryn's ailing father who was staying in the house.

Then there was the emotional testimony from the elderly Ma Coleman, Kathryn's grandmother, whose doctor pushed her into the courtroom in a wheelchair. Kathryn cried as her grandmother corroborated the dinner conversation about the upcoming kidnap and told about the noisy appearance Kelly and Bates had made that night on their way to Paradise with the blindfolded hostage being transferred from one car to the other at her farm.

During a recess, Kathryn convinced her attorney to let her confer with Judge Vaught and make an offer to plead guilty if he would release her mother. The judge threw them out of his chambers telling them he couldn't talk to them about the case. "What in the world are you thinking? Or were you?" he angrily demanded from her lawyer.

Two days into the trial, on October 11, Kathryn swept onto the witness stand, sparing no histrionics. Dressed in black satin, black heels and sheer stockings, and a black hat, she gracefully crossed her legs and began her testimony in an attempt to convince everyone in the courtroom—as well as the nation—of her innocence. Smiling one moment, then dabbing her tears the next, Kathryn portrayed herself in a soft drawl as the real victim. She denied any involvement in the kidnapping, writing the note to Urschel, and being on her uncle's farm when the ransom money was buried. "He always told me not to mess in his business in any way, and I didn't," she told the court. "I had planned to leave Mr. Kelly." Prosecutor Hyde grilled her about the kidnapping. Tearfully, Kathryn told the court of first finding out about the kidnapping and about Kelly threatening to kill Urschel at the ranch:

*I talked to Kelly there by the little house. He said he had a kidnapped man there. I begged him to please release him. He said it was none of my business. He then threatened me. He said they were going to kill him [Urschel]. I begged him not to. [I told him] If you do, I'll tell on you, even if you kill me.*

When Keenan asked, "But Mrs. Kelly, you could have surrendered at any time, couldn't you?" Kathryn replied, "But I didn't know I was wanted." With that, Kathryn was dismissed from the stand.

There was a brief appearance of a so-called handwriting expert who testified on behalf of the government that without any doubt, it had been Kathryn who'd penned the "Ignorant Charles" and other threatening letters, which Kathryn had denied. When shown other writing samples by the defense, the witness offered to appear as a witness on behalf of the Kellys as well. Judge Vaught asked: "You have no hesitancy in appearing here as a witness for the defendants if they give you an opportunity to examine any handwriting they desire you to?"

"No, sir," came the answer. "I have testified for both sides in numerous cases."

However, the judge saw this as a delaying tactic by the defense and would have nothing to do with it. "Well, I am not going to continue this case all fall."

George, who had admitted his own guilt at the time of his arrest, was willing to take all the blame in order to shield Kathryn. Now, with his wife and even his own attorneys trying to place the entire blame on him, he had no hope for acquittal.

In his final argument, Prosecutor Hyde asked the jurors: "How can you believe that this was the demure, loving and fearful wife she pretends to be after hearing that she roamed the country like a millionaire's daughter or wife, buying machine guns? This sweet-smelling geranium.  Do you think she schemed with George and others under threats? I tell you, she was the arch-conspirator."

Hoover had already let his feelings be known that Kathryn's entire line of defense was nothing more than a blatant attempt to shift the blame.

Judge Vaught didn't support her testimony proclaiming her innocence either. Before Kelly had arrived at the Shannon ranch with Urschel, Kathryn had taken her daughter Pauline, now thirteen years old, and Ruth, the twelve-year-old daughter of Boss Shannon from a previous marriage, to her Fort Worth apartment claiming she was lonely and wanted company. In the judge's instructions to the jury, he reminded them of this incident in his astonishing final comments:

*The court would feel it had been cowardly and derelict in duty if it had not pointed out... that the defendant Kathryn was not wholly truthful. This court will not hesitate to tell you that Kathryn Kelly's testimony concerning her removal of the little girls from the Shannon farm near Paradise, Texas, the day Mr. Urschel was brought there did not sound convincing. Her conduct at the Coleman farm... not only is a strong circumstantial point but is convincing to this court that Kathryn knew about the kidnapping and knowingly participated. Other testimony from this defendant is utterly convincing to this court that Kathryn Kelly had criminal knowledge of the abduction conspiracy. However, you can ignore my remarks altogether. They are not binding upon the jury.*

There was no doubt how the verdict would turn out. George's gallant attempt to shield Kathryn by taking the full blame had failed.

In all, the trial took only three days; the jury took less than an hour to reach a verdict. On the morning of October 12, George and Kathryn Kelly were convicted for their roles in the Urschel kidnapping and sentenced to life imprisonment.

International News Service correspondent James L. Kilgallen, who had also covered the Lindbergh baby kidnapping case, described what happened:

*A hushed silence, broken only by the faint whir of motion picture cameras, fell over the crowded courtroom as the verdict was read.*

*Kelly, the man who boasted he can write his name on a wall with machine gun bullets, and his 29-year-old wife who had stuck with him throughout during their hectic married life and criminal career, stood up, side by side.*

*She was pale, her lips tightly compressed and her long slim fingers closing and unclosing. She wore a black silk dress, with red buttons down the front of her waist, and a smart black hat of the latest mode. Kelly, a heavy-set ex-convict, wanted for murder and robbery in several cities, tried to appear nonchalant, but his face was serious as the judge leaned forward. Kelly's dyed hair stood out like a beacon, its yellowish-red hue giving him a grotesque appearance. "Have you anything to say?" asked Judge Vaught in a quiet voice.*

*"No, sir," said Kathryn in a low, tremulous voice. Kelly said nothing….*

*Kathryn's lips trembled as the judge imposed the sentence—the maximum penalty.*

In presenting the sentence, Judge Vaught stated: "The jury found you guilty and the court fully concurs in its verdict. It is therefore the judgment of this court that you be sentenced to the federal penitentiary for the rest of your natural lives. The court is of the opinion that this verdict is fully sustained by the evidence."

Kathryn, clearly angered by the decision, remarked a short time later, "Anyone would have been convicted in this court. If they'd brought my Pekinese in here, he would have gotten a life sentence, too." Then, in a more menacing tone: "They know I've got plenty of friends who will come and get me if I say the word. But if I'm with mother I won't want to escape." Kelly still remained silent, only remarking out of earshot of the judge that the verdict was "no news to me."

As Kelly was led away, Kathryn told him, "Be a good boy." Even though Kathryn and Kelly corresponded throughout the years, she never saw him again. Kelly was thirty-nine years old; Kathryn, twenty-nine.

Berenice and Charles Urschel thanked the judge and shook his hand. Always the gentleman, Urschel told the waiting press: "The government deserves all the credit in the world in this case. I have no feeling of revenge or triumph, but only the highest regard for the officers who worked on the case and the juries which rendered the verdicts."

With the trial now over and as George and Kathryn prepared to spend the rest of their lives in prison, Director Hoover wrote to the director of the Bureau of Prisons making his feelings clear:

*I feel that it is not necessary for me to indicate to you the reputation which Kelly has as an underworld character.... He has boasted that he could not be held in a penitentiary and that he will escape. He has expressed regret that he did not kill Mr. Urschel... and he threatened Mr. Urschel throughout the trial of this kidnapping case.*

*With reference to Kathryn Kelly, I am of the firm opinion that she is a very dangerous criminal.... Kathryn Kelly purchased the machine gun with which her husband, Kelly, was arrested at the time of the kidnapping. She has been identified as the writer of threatening letters received by Mr. Urschel during the trial.*

# CHAPTER 12

## The Fall-out and Other Arrests

Director J. Edgar Hoover had clearly taken a personal interest in the case, planning and following the agents throughout the investigation. Over the next three years, other convictions related to the case took place. Other money changers, people who had sheltered the Kellys, and even Bates' attorney, who had accepted ransom money as part of his fee—all were eventually tracked down, tried, and convicted. The final prison term was handed down the first day of October 1936.

The result led to a total of twenty-one people getting convicted, six of those receiving life sentences. Author Stanley Hamilton states that because the case was so quickly and effectively concluded, it was largely instrumental in bringing about the end of the short-lived but intriguing time in America known as the Gangster Era.

Since the Kellys had no way to pay their attorney, James Mathers, he sued for and was awarded Kathryn's diamond-studded wristwatch and other jewelry, furs, and clothing, as well as George's sixteen-cylinder Cadillac roadster in lieu of legal fees. George had paid four thousand nine hundred forty dollars in cash as a down payment, then paid the remaining thirteen hundred ten dollars in ransom money. Therefore, Urschel felt the car rightfully belonged to him. However, Mathers eventually got to keep the car. He sold various other items, including the watch, along with a letter Kathryn wrote about it, for thirty-five hundred dollars.

Kathryn's Fort Worth home was deeded over to her daughter, Pauline Frye. Pauline also received her mother's other personal effects. Kelly had threatened to bust out of Leavenworth, where he was sentenced, by Christmas. Kathryn told reporters that she still loved him and would see him at Christmas time. "He told me he will break out [at] Christmas and get me out. He always does as he says he will."

Bailey and Bates were flown from the Oklahoma City jail to the military airfield at Fort Leavenworth, Kansas, where they were loaded into an armored car and taken to the Fort Leavenworth Annex, a former U.S. Army disciplinary barracks adjacent to the federal penitentiary. Each man was placed in a solitary confinement cell to prevent any contact with other inmates.

As an added precaution, a special prisoner's railcar fortified with bars and special bulletproof armor plating had been prepared for Kelly's transport to Leavenworth. Inside the car were eight agents armed with machine guns. "Don't worry about me going stir crazy," he told reporters, his hands and feet manacled, as he shuffled from an automobile to the train. "I won't be there long." Under Hoover's directions, the conditions under which he was to be kept upon reaching Leavenworth were even more stringent than those applied to Bailey and Bates:

*[Kelly] should be held incommunicado and no messages or letters should be delivered to or from him. He should be permitted no visits, not even from lawyers, except with the special permission of the Attorney General. He may be seen by the Doctor or by the Chaplain if in your judgment that is wise and safe. I suggest that he be placed in one of the cells in the segregation building; that he be permitted under no circumstances to communicate with other prisoners or to mingle in the yard. He will, of course, be given exercise but in the small exercise yard connected with the segregation unit. He will have regular food, tobacco, books, and newspapers but no other privileges.*

A new penal colony had been proposed that was to house six hundred hard-core prisoners on a remote island called Alcatraz in San Francisco Bay. There was a report that the government was going to make Kelly the first inmate there. "How does that sound to you?" one guard asked, to which Kelly answered, "Listen, the prison at McNeil Island is just as tough. And don't forget, they get away from there. Don't forget it!"

Kelly was written up for "institutional rule violations" shortly after entering Leavenworth and placed in isolation with a restricted diet, and reduced to second grade. In general, he wasn't well liked at Leavenworth by the other inmates and was called "Blabber Mouth" because he talked so much. Kelly remained at Leavenworth until Alcatraz Prison was opened, and in October 1934, after a difficult two-day train ride, he became one of the inaugural inmates, #AZ-117, to do time there along with Albert Bates, #AZ-137, Harvey Bailey, #AZ-139, and one hundred other Leavenworth inmates, as well as another fifty-three prisoners from the federal penitentiary in Atlanta.

After some initial minor disciplinary adjustments, Kelly was considered a model inmate at Alcatraz, receiving the nickname from fellow inmates "Pop Gun Kelly," a somewhat comical, derisive play on Machine Gun Kelly, the violent name that had caused fear throughout the country. He worked in the laundry and was the projectionist at the four movies the inmates were allowed to see each year. When prisoner No. 85, "Scarface" Al Capone who had come from the Atlanta group, organized a prison band, George was the drummer. He became a bible student and even assisted at mass as an "altar boy."

Kelly wrote several apologetic letters during his stay in Alcatraz to Charles Urschel asking him to intercede on his behalf. Urschel chose to ignore the letters. Albert Bates also corresponded with Urschel, but he, too, got nowhere. There was still the issue of the missing ransom money, of which, according to the last FBI statement, only one hundred forty thousand dollars can be accounted for and documented.

George was first eligible for parole in 1948 but declined to file the papers, believing that there was still too much intense ill-feeling about the kidnapping. Also, charges were still pending against him in Oklahoma City for armed robbery, and the FBI had requested notification if he sought parole.

Hoover continued to make it his personal commitment to keep this "mad dog" from being turned loose on society. When informed that Father Joseph M. Clark, a Roman Catholic prison chaplain and personal friend of Cardinal Spellman of New York, was trying to assist in getting Kelly and John Paul Chase, another Alcatraz lifer paroled, Hoover made a note: "Watch closely and endeavor to thwart efforts of this priest who should be attending to his own business instead of trying to turn loose on society such mad dogs." It was this same chaplain who convinced George's youngest son, Bruce Barnes, to re-establish the relationship with his father and visit him in prison. John Paul Chase, who was an associate of Baby-Face Nelson and member of the Dillinger gang and serving a life sentence for the murders of Inspector Samuel P. Cowley and Special Agent H.E. Hollis, was financing Father Clark. J. Edgar Hoover once referred to Chase as "a rat with a patriotic-sounding name."

Warden James V. Bennett would write about Kelly later in his book, *I Chose Prison:*

*Good looking, well mannered, suave of speech, he worked in the Industries Office at Alcatraz, tended to business and gave no trouble. In my conversations with him, Kelly did not spare himself... and felt the shame and embarrassment he had heaped on members of his family. Kelly minimized the part played by his wife and her relatives in the Urschel kidnapping and contended that, while he should pay a heavy penalty, their sentences were too severe and they should be given more consideration. He admitted that his wife knew about and shared his ill-gotten money but was not around when he committed a crime.*

In 1951 Kelly was transferred back to Leavenworth, probably because of his good behavior and declining health, but not without misgivings. When talking to a reporter, he complained: "How the hell did I ever get myself into this fix? I should've stayed with what I knew how to do best—robbing banks."

Even though he had given up the habit of smoking three packs of cigarettes a day, he continued to smoke cigars, especially at night while reading books from the library. He worked in the laundry and the hospital, and occasionally did office work. He died at 12:40 a.m. on the morning of his fifty-fourth birthday in 1954, just before a preliminary hearing had been scheduled to consider his possible parole. He had served twenty-one years in prison.

The prison medical records show his death was due to a "myocardial infarction." An earlier medical report showed that Kelly had been given a Wasserman Test, and that he suffered from an advanced stage of syphilis. When no one claimed the body, Boss Shannon arranged for burial in the Shannon family plot in the small Cottondale Community Cemetery, just outside Paradise, Texas. It is marked by an undistinguished concrete marker bearing a simple inscription with only the year he died and his name, deliberately misspelled, locals say, to protect the grave from souvenir seekers.

Machine Gun Kelly would later become the inspiration for several songs throughout the seventies by such artists as James Taylor, the Angelic Upstarts, Harry Chapin, and Harlem rapper Big L; a dramatic radio episode from the serial program, "G Men", a movie starring Charles Bronson; and a 1974 television film. However, history would remember George, described by author Ellen Poulsen, as a weak man dominated by a strong woman—"that pathetic, hen-pecked husband of Kathryn."

# CHAPTER 13

## Kathryn's Time in Prison

**K**athryn Kelly, who was twenty-nine at the time of her sentencing, and her forty-five-year-old mother, Ora Brooks, sent to the Shelby County Penal Farm in Memphis briefly, were jointly assigned to a federal workhouse facility in Cincinnati, Ohio, because it was "equipped with cells." On October 17, 1933, under the guard of two agents, one deputy, and one female guard, they arrived there by train on track number 4, and not track number 7 as was reported in the papers, for security reasons. It was while Kathryn was at this facility that she discussed with Special Agent E.J. Connelley the idea that "if she were allowed to leave the institution, under conditions indicating that she had escaped; she, then, to be accompanied, or shadowed, by an Agent, she could locate Verne Miller," believed to be the actual perpetrator of the Kansas City Massacre.

Kathryn and her mother would remain together for the next twenty-four years, serving time at several prison facilities and enduring the hardships placed on them. After Cincinnati, they were sent to Milan, Michigan, supposedly for the purpose of interrogating Kathryn about the Lindbergh kidnapping. Special Agent F.J. Blake had written in his report to Director Hoover:

*Mr. Shannon said he was convinced that George and/or Kathryn Kelly could tell the names of those who actually did the kidnapping, basing that statement upon a conversation between himself and Kelly about the time the body of the Lindbergh baby was found. Mr. Shannon said that George Kelly had just come to his place from Chicago, and in discussing the matter Mr. Shannon says that he expressed to Kelly a doubt as to whether the body found was in reality that of the Lindbergh baby, and that the Lindbergh child was still alive; and Kelly said, "No, the baby is dead. I know the men who got it and it is dead. They did not intend to kill it, but dropped it as they were bringing it down the ladder."*

When interviewed by Agent H. Nathan, however, Kathryn was more interested in being an informant, again suggesting that she could be allowed to escape ostensibly, and in an "escape status" she could contact many fugitives the Division would be interested in. "This could not be done by Division Agents inasmuch as it is necessary to go to a certain place and leave word to have the fugitives call, etc. that a parole status would not give her the opportunity she desired because she would be looked upon with suspicion," Agent Nathan wrote of his conversation with Kathryn in his report to Director Hoover. However, Hoover wasn't interested, although the information Kathryn did give Agent Nathan eventually led to her receiving radio and exercise privileges and the right to correspond with her daughter, Pauline. She was still kept in solitary confinement. Her mother was as well.

Kathryn also spent time at a federal prison facility at Seagoville, Texas, and later in California on Terminal Island. A largely artificial island located in Los Angeles County, she continued to pursue her interest in writing, something she had done the previous decade. In December 1940, she had reflected on a life of crime and its futility:

*We realize that every 'feminine fluff' beneath our roof carries within her heart a full quota of loneliness, grief and mental suffering. None of us like to do 'time'. It isn't play, it is sapping three hundred and sixty-five days filled with golden opportunities slipping away year by year, each day gone forever from the span of life. The drabness, the necessary discipline attached to an institution pulls at the vital organs of living twenty-four hours each day. The Government can never fashion from steel and stone a prison that will mean 'home' to any of its inmates.*

At one point, Kathryn wrote to George reminding him that she was superstitious and telling him she wanted a divorce. Her motivation wasn't clear, but some believe it was because she felt her chances of getting paroled would be better. She wrote:

*I find that I am completely cured of any craving for un-legitimate luxuries and my sincere hopes and plans for the future are of a sane, balanced mode in living. I'll never change on that viewpoint. I have gone through hell and still am plainly speaking, seeing mother as a daily reminder of my own mistake. The mistake was my love, and marriage to you.*

A short time later, however, she changed her mind, telling him to forget that she ever mentioned the word "divorce," and that she loved him. Some of her poetry expresses that strong love she had, presumably for George:

*In groping for cheerful words a poem to write –*

*I find I cannot grasp the gay in life tonight –*

*Years loom so long, fate is a devil, made with glee,*

*Tossing prison arrows into the soul of me –*

*My heart is numb, yet aching with the need of you.*

*Grim, stark sadness dims everything I try to do,*

*That banner in courage I carried fell apart –*

*The want of you is like no other thing, dear heart.*

Kathryn also stayed in contact with her father, James Emory Brooks, who told her that he had contacted the Governor of Tennessee in an effort to "get her off."

During her time at the federal prison facility on Terminal Island, she became assistant editor of a prison newspaper, *The Terminal Island Gull,* to which she contributed poetry and articles.

Kathryn eventually ended up in a minimum-security federal prison for female inmates located in Alderson, West Virginia. Following a reformatory model for prisons with no fenced grounds or armed guards, this one hundred fifty-nine-acre prison offered education in a boarding school atmosphere. More recently, in 2004 it would be nicknamed "Camp Cupcake" by the news media when Martha Stewart was sentenced to a five-month term there for her involvement in the ImClone insider trading affair.

In June 1958, while serving time at Alderson as prisoner No. 5485, Kathryn got the name of an attorney from one of her fellow inmates, Mildred Elizabeth Gillars, better known by American troops serving in the European theater as "Axis Sally."

Kathryn's new attorney, James J. Laughlin, was able to obtain a reopening of the proceeding in the same court in which their trials had been held. He had first tried to get Kathryn and her mother paroled, but without success. "Urschel, I am told, was prepared to spend one million dollars, if necessary, to keep Mrs. Kelly and her mother in prison," he said in a *New York Times* interview.

At issue was the testimony of handwriting expert D.C. Patterson who claimed that the Urschel ransom notes as well as some of the threatening letters had been written by Kathryn; and he reputed the original trial judge's refusal to grant her the right to have the letters examined by another expert, who in all probability would have disputed Patterson's testimony. This was made even more evident when a long-suppressed internal memorandum dated September 23, 1933, written by the FBIs own handwriting expert, Charles A. Appel, offered the opinion that the letters were not written by Kathryn. Appel followed up his initial memorandum with another laboratory report that stated: "I am still of the opinion that she did not write these letters."

In addition to the handwriting argument, Laughlin brought forth other allegations. He challenged the policy of keeping Kathryn on bread and water to "weaken her resolve," something Agent Nathan had requested according to an internal FBI memo, and other mistreatment measures, such as keeping a bright light on in her cell during the night to prevent sleep, and not giving her the same privileges afforded other prisoners, such as the use of a radio and being allowed to exercise.

He made the charge of "inadequate assistance of counsel, use of testimony known to be false, denial of compulsory service of process, and conduct of the trial in an atmosphere which prevented a fair and impartial trial," more than likely referring to the use of film projectors in the courtroom during the trial proceedings themselves.

Judge Vaught was now retired, and the new judge on the case, Judge William R. Wallace, ordered the FBI to produce its files on the Urschel case. However, much to his surprise, he was informed by U.S. District Attorney Paul Cress that no transcript of the Kellys' 1933 trial could be found. They eventually located the faded handwritten transcriptions of the trial that had been prepared by court reporter B. Rule Simpson at the time, but he had used the old-style Pitman shorthand system, and not the later Gregg system or newly emerging stenotype machine. No one could decipher the notes.

The aged original court reporter agreed to help, but the records eventually transcribed were incomplete. With these partial notes and an "agreed narrative statement of evidence" as the backdrop, the reopened proceeding covered a frustrating six days of rambling testimony, forgotten memories and vague recollections.

Many of the original witnesses were dead; others were now in their seventies or eighties. Efforts to locate the Arnolds proved futile and only added to the drama as various unsubstantiated and outlandish stories surfaced that Geraldine had become a movie actress in Hollywood under the name of Virginia Lane, that she had become a nun and was living in Rome, Italy, and that she was living with a man in California. Charles Urschel and Ernest Earl Kirkpatrick were both subpoenaed by Kathryn's attorney but spent six days registered incognito in a nearby hotel waiting for the call to testify that never came.

The climax of the six-day hearing—which lasted twice as long as Kathryn's trial twenty-five years earlier—came swiftly after a noon recess. Shortly before the noon hour, Judge Wallace gave U.S. District Attorney Paul Cress a final ultimatum to produce the FBI reports which were the basis for the nation's first trial under the Lindbergh kidnapping law. Wallace based his ruling that the government must produce the files to show whether or not defense attorneys in the Urschel case were under investigation during the trial and therefore intimidated by threats of prosecution for receiving ransom money.

When the hearing resumed, Cress asked permission to present a motion for a continuance. Judge Wallace refused. Cress then announced he would be unable to produce the FBI reports, which he said was based on orders from U.S. Attorney General William P. Rogers. James J. Laughlin, attorney for the two women, immediately rose to his feet and requested a re-trial.

Displeased by the government's stonewalling and lack of cooperation that bordered on contempt-of-court, Judge Wallace granted the women's petition for a rehearing, and as a result, Kathryn and her mother, Ora Shannon, each were conditionally released from prison on a ten thousand dollar bond, pending an appeal. U.S. marshals in the courtroom waved down a brief handclapping demonstration which followed Judge Wallace's announcement. At first dazed, both women then burst into tears.

For the first time in twenty-five years behind bars, on the evening of June 16, 1958, Kathryn and Ora walked down the steps of the federal building in Oklahoma City as free citizens, pending any new hearing.

The first thing Kathryn did was place a long-distance call to the warden at Alderson: "I'll never be back," she said. Both women had something to say to the press. Kathryn wanted to take her mother to "a good hospital, just to be checked out." She had suffered several heart attacks while in prison. "We have kept up with the atomic bombs and the sputniks and all of that," Ora told reporters. "We have studied and prepared for this day so we could step right out into the world and take our places."

Kathryn and her mother had been together in the same cottage at Alderson for the past sixteen years. They worked together in the flower shop for a time, and later transferred to the garment shop. Kathryn's mother revealed proudly, "She's [Kathryn] been the secretary to the 'big boss' in the garment shop... she's been the bookkeeper, shipping clerk, and the works.... She won't have any trouble. She can do so many things." Kathryn seemed a little less certain. "I guess the thing that impressed me most on my first trip out was the fast traffic. I was honestly afraid to cross the streets."

Faced with the uncertainty of how they were going to make enough money to live on, Kathryn came up with the idea that the two of them could tour coast to coast making personal appearances to tell their side of the story. Her attorney, however, convinced her that with the case technically still open and pending, it would be better to leave things as they stood.

Another year passed and things continued to remain in limbo until a higher court on appeal directed that the hearing should be continued "on its merits," and Wallace's original ruling releasing the women was reversed. However, a short time later, seventy-four-year-old Wallace was killed in a head-on automobile crash near Oklahoma City. With others who had been involved in the case also gone, the case against Kathryn and Ora remained at an impasse.

One of the issues that had been brought up by Laughlin on behalf of Kathryn and Ora was the "Roman holiday" atmosphere that had existed during the first trial. In refuting the testimony of Herbert Hyde and other government witnesses that "photographs were taken only at recess and before and after court, not while court was actually in session," he produced a story by *North Star* photographer C.J. Kaho:

> *On the first day of the trial, all photographers were called in the Judge's chambers and told the court room is yours – you may make a picture any time, in any place in the court room, while the court is in session – we want all the publicity we can get on this case.*

The story continued:

> *From the first day, the federal building, especially the ninth floor, was a veritable arsenal, no place you could look or turn but that a machine gun was facing you…. The first two days seemed like a dream, here I was making pictures from the judge's bench, practically popping flash bulbs in his ear, shooting down in the court room, and every shot expecting someone to come and get me, for violating a federal law. Nothing happened…. The picture of the day was that line up. I made it standing in the witness chair.*

Throughout her confinement, Kathryn had been placed on a bread and water diet. At one point the prison doctor had been called in to administer to Kathryn. She was so weak, having had nothing substantial to eat, she was unable to hold down any food. The doctor hand fed her. Afterwards, he wrote the warden a letter threatening to resign as prison doctor unless Kathryn was fed a proper diet. Although this story was according to Kathryn's own sworn affidavit, Laughlin was able to produce two notes written by prison physicians who had examined Kathryn and add them to his arsenal of weapons against the government.

Laughlin also charged that the FBI had conducted investigations of the attorneys at the first trial to intimidate them into putting on a less than vigorous defense.

Afraid that embarrassing, at the very least if not actually damaging, testimony against the government was very possible regarding these charges as well as the evidence relating to the handwritten letters, the FBI chose to let the case lapse rather than release its files which included the suppressed report by another FBI handwriting expert, Charles A. Appel, who stated: "The handwriting on the letters to the *Oklahoman* and to Urschel is not identical with that of Mrs. Kelly.... A comparison of the signatures of George R. Kelly on three fingerprint cards with those on these letters indicates that he may have written these letters...." This finding wouldn't become public until 1970 when it was published by William W. Turner, a former FBI agent who had been fired after ten years of service. As a result of the FBI refusing to produce their twenty-five-year-old records, Kathryn Kelly and Ora Brooks remained free.

Kathryn was given a job as a two hundred dollar-a-month bookkeeping job at the Oklahoma County Home and Hospital in Oklahoma City with the promise of a pension. Her mother also worked there as a nurse assisting the elderly. The one condition of their employment was that "Kay," as she was called at her workplace, and Ora not discuss the case. Through it all, Kathryn steadfastly stuck to her story of innocence.

During the time that Kathryn spent in prison, public opinion went against her, forcing her to live under a stream of false identifications. E.E. Kirkpatrick, Urschel's friend who delivered the ransom, blamed Kathryn in the kidnap plot in his book, *Crimes' Paradise.* "She was a manipulator, a murderess, an instigator of a ring of kidnappers; a dragon-lady responsible for the downfall of George 'Machine Gun' Kelly." Hoover, never one for holding back his pejorative opinion of Kathryn, declared that "she [Kathryn] is a hundred times more vicious and dangerous than a man... she acts with cold brutality seldom found in a man." Concerned over Kathryn's possible parole, Charles Urschel expressed his own opinion, "... she is far more to be feared than George Kelly." Kelly's son wrote in his book, "She was a born con artist, never truly accepting responsibility for her role in the Urschel affair.... She was without question the dominating impetus, the plotter, the instigator, the brains behind the entire Urschel scheme." More recently, in discussing his work of fiction, crime writer Ace Atkins refers to Kathryn as the Lady Macbeth of Depression-era crime.

Ellen Poulsen describes in her book, *Don't Call Us Molls,* the unglamorous life and hardships forced on the women involved with gangsters during this period, and in light of their sad reality, they avoided publicity. "It wasn't until after the Kansas City Massacre in 1933 that they were taken seriously enough to interrogate with the same force and brutality used on male prisoners. The primitive use of bright lights and sleep deprivation advanced to the denial of constitutional rights. A woman could be held for up to two weeks without regular sleep, food, or telephone access to an attorney. She could be punched, have her hair pulled, and burned with cigarettes. Verbal abuse in the form of insults and racial and ethnic slurs was frequent."

It is unknown how much of this treatment Kathryn was exposed to, if any. There is no question that in the beginning just following her arrest, Katherine seemed to relish the attention, and it was through her that Hoover elaborated on the idea of a woman with superior criminal intelligence. She changed, however, from the cocky, self-assured fashion plate when she first entered prison to a more subdued, somewhat nervous middle-aged woman, veiled in black, when she was finally allowed to leave the guarded walls of prison and re-enter a life of freedom. Only a remnant of that quick, bright smile she had flashed for photographers and reporters at the beginning of her trial twenty-five years earlier remained. More mature and less impulsive after having spent a quarter of a century behind bars, with no desire for publicity, it isn't any wonder that when contacted in 1962, Kathryn expressed concern: "Why can't they just leave us alone? I'm afraid I'll lose this job if this constant barrage of publicity keeps up... I was just a young farm girl when I met Kelly back in 1930... I wasn't used to all the money, cars and jewelry George offered me... Any farm girl would have been swept off her feet same as I was."

In the summer of 1963, once again the case was revived. Luther Bohannon, nominated on August 18, 1961, by John F. Kennedy to a joint appointment to seats on the Western, Eastern, and Northern Districts of Oklahoma, all vacated at the death of William R. Wallace, disapproved of the manner in which the case had been allowed to remain pending without any judicial resolution. He mentioned to the Justice Department that Mrs. Kelly and Mrs. Shannon should either be placed on parole or that the hearings called for by the decision of the Court of Appeals should be held. However, he went along with the recommendation of the Department of Justice to leave things as they were and, in effect, expunging the convictions of both women since Judge Wallace's initial order, which was never annulled, stated: "The motions of these two just-referred to defendants to vacate and set aside judgment of conviction and for new trial are hereby sustained." This, at last, was the final word.

Ora died in 1980 at the age of 92, five years before Kathryn, at the suburban Oklahoma City home they shared. Kathryn died in Tulsa on May 28, 1985, as Wisconsin native "Lera Cleo Kelly," a contrived identity, who lived at a west Tulsa nursing home. She was 81. Kathryn's granddaughter, Elaine Neely, who helped take care of her in her later years, said she seldom discussed the case and never mentioned any proposed deal with the government—referring to Kathryn's attempt to get the government to show leniency toward her and her mother in exchange for George.

The Oklahoma Osteopathic Hospital still exists today near the Arkansas River, where Kathryn spent her last days alone and anonymous. Kathryn and Ora are buried side by side in the Tecumseh Cemetery located in Pottawatomie County near Oklahoma City, Oklahoma.

# CHAPTER 14

## A Final Word

So much has been written about Kathryn's involvement in the Charles Urschel kidnapping and the subsequent trials, most of it speculation. In order to understand Kathryn and her motivation, one must also remember the times in which she lived. It was the age of Prohibition, the Great Depression, and the Dirty Thirties. It was the "Gangster Era."

No one was left untouched by the poor state of the economy, not only in this country but around the world. For most, they got by. But for a few, it created an intangible driving need that couldn't be explained, and was only satisfied by what would become known as the Mid-West Crime Wave. Although the period itself lasted just a few short years, it left behind a legacy of personalities—the "Public Enemies" sometimes viewed as notorious, but other times seen as tragic victims—that would be etched into the annals of American criminal history forever: John Dillinger, Pretty Boy Floyd, Baby Face Nelson, Alvin Creepy Karpis, Ma Barker and the Barker Gang, Bonnie and Clyde—as well as Machine Gun Kelly and his wife, Kathryn.

The participants of the Mid-West Crime Wave gave J. Edgar Hoover the impetus to propel his fledgling Bureau of Investigation, then a small division of the U. S. Justice Department, into the Federal Bureau of Investigation we know today.

In addition, the Mid-West Crime Wave allowed Hollywood to produce gut-wrenching action motion pictures of the era with the criminals being romanticized by some of the biggest names in the motion picture industry such as Warren Beatty, Faye Dunaway, James Cagney, Shelly Winters, Robert DeNiro, Mark Harmon, Warren Oates, Martin Sheene, Mickey Rooney, and Richard Dreyfuss.

In early 1934 while in prison, Kathryn wrote what was purported to be her life story: *History of My Checkered Career* by Mrs. Kathryn "Machine-Gun" Kelly Barnes. In this autobiography, she tried to explain her feelings:

*... as I grew older it became harder for me to be content. I longed for new faces, for a larger city. I was restless and discontented....*

Then she talks about the joy she felt—for a while—after her child was born. Using a fictitious name:

> *... but when June was a little past a year old, the old unrest and discontentment began to haunt me. I fought many and many a battle in the depths of my heart then. Something seemed to be calling and calling to me from outside my little world. I grew unhappier as the days passed on. I began finding fault with every little thing... so at last I just had to get away.*

Things seemed to change for Kathryn once she met George. She felt she had at last found the fulfillment and joy in life that had for so long been missing:

> *Months flew by into years – years of gay luxurious fun – to Florida and Cuba in the winter and one gay resort after another – something amusing constantly. We never settled down but always had money and spent it daily and freely. [I see us] now as pawns of an inverted environment and fate, just like two bits of seawood [sic] tossing about so busily engaged in guzzling down gulps of pleasure. We never thought of a tomorrow, a butterfly existence; we never had time to be serious, eternally gay.*

Just like the others who fell victim to the call of danger, excitement, and a life that was more thrilling than what was available in reality, Kathryn pursued that butterfly existence with an energy and determination that matched even the most desperate of criminals. For a while, she had it in her grasp. In the end, however, she would discover that the life she so vigorously sought was just as ephemeral as the life of a butterfly. Perhaps her own words best summarize the character of this complex woman:

*I have known the ecstasy of extreme happiness. I have experienced the extreme of despair and now my proud head is bent low, drinking deeply of my life's most bitter cup and I've placed the bittars in that cup with my own hands…. My heart is an open wound, emptily aching with the knowledge of the life I have wanted and the loss of all I hold dear. I have only memories for company, memories of what might have been… haunted memories of the wasted years I spent, to recall with a prayer for forgiveness to an ignored and almost forgotten God for another chance. I have known life and love, I have known death and disaster, been the friend of foals, succumbed to sin, been not unacquainted with crime, loved and lost, smiled and wept, but now, God is my only Master.*

ౡఠ  ౡఠ  ౡఠ  ౡఠ

# EPILOGUE

## Charles Frederick Urschel

Charles Urschel and his wife, Berenice, moved from Oklahoma City in 1945 and relocated in San Antonio where he headed the Slick-Urschel Oil Company. They sold their house to former Oklahoma governor and later U.S. Senator Robert S. Kerr. After a lengthy illness, Charles Urschel died on September 26, 1970, four months after Berenice.

## Berenice Frates Slick Urschel

Berenice Slick Urschel continued doing philanthropy work and along with other family members made sizeable donations to Thomas Baker Slick, Jr.'s various visionary scientific research and education foundations. Tom Slick, Jr., died in 1962 in a plane crash, four years after founding the Mind Science Foundation. The Foundation's work of studying human consciousness continues today. As a side note, forty years after that fateful night of the kidnapping, Berenice wrote a letter to Director Hoover with a copy to Hon. Carl Albert, M.C.:

> *Dear Mr. Hoover,*
>
> *Enclosed copy of Tulsa Daily World recalls very vividly the Charles Urschel case. I was told by our Federal Judge to call you. It was after midnight but I called and you told me to wait until two of your men from Shawnee arrived.*
>
> *Forty years ago seems like only a few years. As usual, Charles got back safely and the kidnaper went to jail.*
>
> *All this is to try to tell you how sincerely I wish you all the happiness you so richly deserve.*
>
> *Very truly yours,*
>
> *Berenice Urschel*

## Ernest Earl Kirkpatrick

Friend of Charles Urschel who delivered the $200,000 ransom in Kansas City authored two books about the abduction. He was eighty-six when he died of an apparent heart attack in April 1968 while on a business trip in Tulsa.

## Pauline Elizabeth Frye

Pauline Elizabeth Frye, Kathryn's daughter, "grew up to be a fine professional woman with high moral standards and a commitment to serve humanity," according to Bruce Barnes. Following the verdicts, Pauline was taken in by an aunt, Mrs. Pearl Hopkins, in Asher, Oklahoma, where she eventually finished secondary school with good marks. Dreaming of becoming a school teacher, she earned enough money doing odd jobs to start college at East Central State Teachers College in Ada, Oklahoma (renamed East Central University in 1974), but that quickly ran out. Throughout this time, she had continued to correspond with Judge Vaught about the possibility of parole for her mother and grandmother, and even petitioned the court for the return of her mother's jewelry and furs, thinking she could sell them in order to finance her education. Receiving no encouragement from him regarding a parole or the return of Kathryn's things held in evidence, Judge Vaught did write to her regarding the matter of her education. He had made arrangements for her to continue her education:

> *I am making arrangements... to furnish your room and board, buy your books and to pay your college fees connected with your work as a student. The only other expenses, which you would incur in addition to these, are for your clothes and personal expenses. I will arrange to pay you $50 on account for the clothes.*
>
> *I do not care for any publicity to be given this matter. Nobody but you, your aunt, Dr. Lenscheid [president of the school], and I will*

*know anything about it. Dr. Lenscheid will send all of the bills directly to me....*

Pauline went on to complete her college and received a degree in teaching, all the while corresponding with Judge Vaught. She later married Olin Glenn Horn in 1938 and they had two children. Pauline (Fry) Horn died December 31, 2005, and is buried in Tulsa, Oklahoma.

Only recently was it discovered in the private archives of Judge Vaught that Vaught was merely the go-between for the real benefactor. An undated handwritten cover note was attached to the collection of correspondence between Judge Vaught and Pauline stating:

> *The enclosed data has to do with Pauline Frye, daughter of Catherine Kelley [sic], convicted in this court for participation in Urschel kidnapping. Pauline was a student in Teachers College at Ada, and after her mother went to the penitentiary, all of Pauline's expenses were paid by Mr. Urschel but he did not want it known and hence the payments were made through me. – E.S.V.*

## Robert K. Green Boss Shannon

Robert K.G. Boss Shannon, after serving eleven years, received a pardon from President Franklin D. Roosevelt in 1944, the reason given owing to Shannon's ill health. Shannon returned to his ranch in Paradise, Texas, hoping that oil would be discovered on his property. It never was. It is reported that he made at least one bus trip to West Virginia in order to visit his wife, Ora, and his stepdaughter, Kathryn, who were incarcerated there at Alderson. Boss Shannon died on Christmas Day 1956 in a Bridgeport, Texas, hospital. The government wouldn't give Ora or Kathryn permission to attend the service; however, it was reported by locals that Boss' wife and stepdaughter both returned to Paradise after Boss Shannon died to tend to the partials of land bequeathed to them at his death, which were eventually sold. Either way, there was a large spray of red roses on the casket with a ribbon saying "Husband." Boss Shannon is buried in the Cottondale Cemetery between his first two wives, Icye and Maude, and two graves over from George Barnes Kelly.

## Harvey John Bailey

Harvey Bailey, the only person convicted who didn't actually participate in the kidnapping. While serving time in Dallas County jail, he apparently was so well liked by the guards that trusty Nelson Norris often played his guitar for him while other inmates danced the jig. Two of Bailey's favorite tunes were "Birmingham Jail" and "Silver-Haired Daddy of Mine." A reporter from "The Dallas Dispatch" would write, "Despite the fact Harvey Bailey was considered one of the most dangerous killers ever held in Dallas County jail, he was feted and entertained with an attitude that bordered on hero worship." Bailey was paroled from Leavenworth in 1961, but then was immediately re-arrested by Kansas State authorities for a bank robbery he had committed in 1933. Bailey was sent to the Kansas Penitentiary until 1965 when his sentence was commuted by the governor. He spent his last years in Joplin, Missouri, where, with the financial assistance of E.E. Kirkpatrick and Charles Urschel, he lived in the YMCA, and worked as a cabinetmaker. As part of the financial arrangements, he also assisted E.E. Kirkpatrick in writing a book about his life. Bailey died in March 1979 at the age of 91.

## Albert Bates

Albert Bates died on Alcatraz on July 4, 1948.

## Langford Poland Ramsey

Langford Ramsey, Kelly's former brother-in-law, was disbarred and served thirty months in the Atlanta Penitentiary for complicity in the kidnapping

## Walter R. Jarrett

Charles Urschel's friend and other kidnap victim, Walter Jarrett, was accused by Kelly and Bates as being the "finger man" in the kidnapping, and for his part he was to receive twenty-five thousand dollars. They described in detail how Jarrett would park his Pierce Arrow car on the side of Urschel's home if all was clear, or in front of his home if it was not. This story was corroborated by Kathryn. Later, however, Kelly and Bates both denied Jarrett's involvement.

The reason they had implicated him was to prevent him from testifying against Kelly. Jarrett and his wife moved to Midland, Texas, in 1938 where he died at the age of sixty on February 16, 1947.

## Armon Crawford "Potatoes" Shannon

Armon Shannon's probation was lifted in 1939 for good behavior. He returned to Wise County where he eventually married two more times and had seven children. He died in 1968 at the age of fifty-seven. He is buried in the Cottondale family plot near his father and Kelly.

## Judge Edgar Sullins Vaught.

Judge Vaught was elected to the Oklahoma Hall of Fame in 1941 and served as chief judge from 1949 to 1956, assuming senior status on April 22, 1956. Vaught served in that capacity until his death, in 1959.

## The Arnolds

Luther William Arnold, in his early forties at the time of the Urschel kidnapping trials, eventually wound up around the Long Beach, California, area with a long arrest record for forged checks, spousal abuse, selling liquor to the Indians, and white slave trafficking. He reportedly died around 1944 in southern California. Flossie Marie is believed to have died at a Veterans Home in 1963 at the age of eighty. It is believed that Geraldine married and took her husband's name. Even though the FBI attempted to get them deposed at the reopened 1958 proceeding, the Arnolds could not be located.

## George Barnes, Jr. (Sonny)

Bruce Barnes writes that his older brother never forgave his father for the physical and mental abuse he suffered as a child—or for the notoriety that was inflicted on the family. George, Jr., married and had five children, three of whom died from muscular dystrophy. On June 16, 1989, George, Jr., died of a massive heart attack while on his way to his grandson's graduation.

## Bruce Barnes

Bruce Barnes, younger son and biographer of his father, George Machine Gun Kelly, retired after thirty-five years as a lamp designer and manufacturer. He lives on a horse ranch in California.

## Cassey Earl Coleman and Will Casey

Both Coleman and Casey were indicted at Dallas, Texas, on October 4, 1933, charged with harboring a fugitive and conspiracy. On October 17, 1933, Coleman entered a plea of guilty and was sentenced to serve one year and one day at Leavenworth. Casey was sentenced to serve two years, also at Leavenworth.

## J.C. Tichemor

J.C. Tichemor was indicted at Jackson, Tennessee, on charges of conspiracy and harboring and concealing a fugitive. On October 21, 1933, he was sentenced to serve two years and six months imprisonment.

## Louise Magness

On February 22, 1934, Louise Magness was indicted at Fort Worth, Texas and charged with harboring George and Kathryn Kelly. On April 30, 1934, she entered a plea of guilty and was sentenced to serve one year and one day in the Federal Industrial Institution for Women at Alderson, West Virginia.

## Others

On December 14, 1934, the following persons were indicted by a federal grand jury at Oklahoma City, Oklahoma, charging them with conspiracy to violate the Kidnapping Statute: Ben B. Laska, James C. Mathers, Clara Feldman, Edward Feldman, and Alvin Scott. On December 17, 1934, Clara Feldman entered a plea of guilty to the indictment. Edward Feldman and Alvin Scott pleaded guilty on January 2, 1935. Alvin Scott, Clara Feldman, and Edward Feldman were sentenced on June 15, 1935, to serve five years each in a federal penitentiary. These sentences were suspended for five years, and each was placed on probation.

James C. Mathers and Ben Laska were tried in Federal Court at Oklahoma City, Oklahoma, on June 10, 1935. On June 14, 1935, Mathers was acquitted by a directed verdict. On June 15, 1935, Laska was sentenced to serve ten years in a federal penitentiary. Laska was released on a $10,000 bond pending an appeal. The U.S. Circuit Court of Appeals for the 10th Circuit at Denver, Colorado on March 27, 1936, rendered a decision affirming the District Court at Oklahoma City. Laska surrendered to the U.S. Marshal at Oklahoma City on August 1, 1936, and was removed to the U.S. Penitentiary at Leavenworth, Kansas, on the same date.

Mrs. Mollie O. Bert, a Denver, Colorado, attorney, furnished untruthful testimony during the trials of Laska. As a result of this testimony, a complaint was filed against Mrs. Bert at Oklahoma City on June 15, 1936, charging her with perjury. She was released on a $5,000 bond after a plea of not guilty. On October 1, 1936, Mrs. Bert withdrew her plea of not guilty and entered a plea of *nolle contendere* and was sentenced on the same date to serve one year and one day imprisonment, which sentence was suspended pending good behavior for one year.

In all, twenty-one persons were convicted in this case with six life sentences. The other sentences totaled fifty-eight years, two months, and three days.

## The Missing Ransom

The missing ransom has been the subject of mystery for the last seventy years, due in part to Albert Bates' stubborn refusal to give any clues to its whereabouts. "You'll never find the money. I've buried it," Bates claimed while in prison. Of the $200,000 in twenty dollar bills paid as ransom, the FBI was able to account for $123,394.50 of the ransom money and money obtained in exchange for ransom notes, as well as other sums that were spent or disposed of by the subjects. It is alleged that $45,205.50 has never been recovered and is assumed to be buried somewhere in the hills near Oklahoma City.

# NOTES OF INTEREST

- The Thompson machine gun that Kathryn bought as a gift for George from J. Kar at the Wolf & Klar pawn shop remained on display for many years at the Fort Worth, Texas, Police Academy. Other items, such as George's leather money belt, various pistols taken from George, the assortment of vessels in which the Urschel ransom money was buried, the wig worn by Kathryn, and the chain used in restraining Charles Urschel are displayed in exhibit cases at the Division of Investigations and the Federal Bureau of Investigation museum.

- President Lyndon Johnson signed an Executive Order waiving mandatory retirement on the behalf of J. Edgar Hoover.

- The Urschel home was described as a "mansion." The Oklahoma County Assessor's records state that the home contains 6,330 square feet. The Oklahoma City Historical Preservation Commission's marker on NW 18th indicates that it was built in 1923, and originally owned by Tom Slick. It would later be owned by US Senator Robert S. Kerr.

- Information that Kathryn tried to work out a deal with the government, whereby she and her mother would be given leniency in exchange for George Kelly, has been brought into question. Luther Arnold testified that Kathryn had asked him to arrange a meeting at the Skirvin Plaza Hotel between Kathryn's attorney Sam Sayers and the Oklahoma attorneys representing her mother to work out the deal. He also testified that he had overheard Kathryn and George discussing it, and that George had told her, "Well go ahead and make your dicker and when you get it made, let me know. I'm willing to go, but you know I can't go to them and do any dickering." An undated telegram, on file at a National Archives warehouse in Fort Worth, from the U.S. Attorney in Fort Worth to U.S. Attorney Herbert K. Hyde of Oklahoma City reports an "offer" by Kathryn's attorney Sam Sayers to surrender Kelly in return for leniency for Kathryn and her mother. By September 7, Hyde had passed the offer along to Joseph B. Keenan, the special assistant attorney general who had been charged with heading the government's war against gangsters and racketeers. In a letter to Hyde, Keenan flatly rejected any deal which would deprive the government of the right to deal with Kelly, Bates and Bailey as it saw fit, even to the point of seeking the death penalty under the new kidnapping law. But, Keenan added that if the government could get Kelly and the ransom money, "I am hoping that Judge Vaught could see his way clear to being very lenient to Mrs. Shannon and Mrs. Kelly, even to the point of absolute release... if we had a free hand to deal with Kelly, Bates and Bailey as the facts justify." This, of course, never happened.

- In October 1959, WTOP-TV aired "Sounds of Eden," a portrayal of the Urschel kidnapping. Robert Kennedy, former counsel for the McClellan Committee, commented briefly at the introduction and conclusion of the play concerning the need for citizen participation in combating the problem of organized crime.

- Kathryn owned a pure-bred Pekinese, registered by the American Kennel Club, female, and red and black in color with a mask. Its name was *Ching A Wee*. Its sire was *Po-Chu*; its dam was *Chu Waa*. She called it "Sammie."

- John Edgar Hoover (January 1, 1895 – May 2, 1972) was appointed director of the Bureau of

Investigation in 1924 and was instrumental in founding the FBI in 1935, where he remained director until his death in 1972 at age 77. Hoover is credited with building the FBI into a larger crime-fighting agency, and with instituting a number of modernizations to police technology, such as a centralized fingerprint file and forensic laboratories. In 1924, an act of congress established the Identification Division of the FBI. The IACP's National Bureau of Criminal Identification and the US Justice Department's Bureau of Criminal Identification consolidated to form the nucleus of the FBI fingerprint files. The kidnapping of Charles Urschel was partially solved using fingerprints, but not in the normal fashion. Urschel was held captive by George Machine Gun Kelly and his partner in a farm house for several days in 1933. After receiving a ransom of $200,000, the two released Urschel, but not before he left his fingerprints on every item in the house he could get his hands on. The authorities were able to convict the two kidnappers based primarily on this evidence, which proved that the businessman had been held in the house.

- Kathryn had two insurance policies at the time of her incarceration. One was an endowment policy for fifteen hundred dollars, taken out with Metropolitan Insurance Company in 1925. The other was a life insurance policy in the amount of two thousand dollars taken out with United Benefit Life Insurance Company in 1927. Her daughter, Pauline, was the beneficiary in both policies.

- Prior to the Urschel kidnapping case, it wasn't unusual for members of the FBI and other law enforcement agencies to keep "souvenirs" that had been collected from a particular case. However, in this case, FBI Director Hoover insisted on everything being kept in order to properly display it in special exhibits at the FBI headquarters.

- The development of the Thompson submachine gun and its use by gangsters— especially during the 1929 St. Valentine's Day Massacre when seven people were killed— reportedly led to the 1934 National Firearms Act and the public pressure for gun control in the United States.

- Until 1935, the FBI officially bore the title of the Division of Investigation, U.S. Department of Justice.

# BIBLIOGRAPHY

## Books

Barnes, Bruce. *Machine Gun Kelly: To Right a Wrong.* Perris, California: Tipper Publications, 1991.

Cooper, Courtney Ryley. *Ten Thousand Public Enemies:* Foreword by J. Edgar Hoover. Boston: Little, Brown & Co., 1935.

Hamilton, Stanley. *Machine Gun Kelly's Last Stand.* Kansas: University Press of Kansas, 2003.

Helmer, William J. and Rick Mattix. *Public Enemies: America's Criminal Past, 1919-1940.* New York: Facts on File, Inc., 1998.

_____ *The Complete Public Enemy Almanac.* Tennessee: Cumberland House, 2007.

Hoover, J. Edgar. *Persons in Hiding.* Foreword by Courtney Ryley Cooper. Boston: Little, Brown and Co., 1938.

Karpis, Alvin with Bill Trent. *The Alvin Karpis Story*. New York: Coward, McCann & Geoghegan, Inc., 1971.

May, Allan. Gangland Gotham: New York's Notorious Mob Bosses. New Hampshire: Greenwood, 2009.

Poulsen, Ellen. *Don't Call Us Molls: Women of the John Dillinger Gang.* New York: Clinton Cook Publishing Corp., 2002.

Quimby, Myron J. *The Devil's Emissaries.* New Jersey: A.S. Barnes & Co., 1969.

Sifakis, Carl. *The Encyclopedia of American Crime.* New York: Smithmark Publishers, 1992.

Toland, John. *The Dillinger Days.* New York: Random House, 1963.

**Newspapers and Pamphlets**

U.S. Bureau of Prisons Archives, Washington, D.C.

    "The Alderson Sage"

    "Federal Industrial Institution for Women"

    "Federal Reformatory for Women"

The National Archives at Kansas City

"They're Not Going to Get Me"

Famous Cases & Criminals

"George Machine Gun Kelly"

The Gull

"We Guild the Lily"

"George Machine Gun Kelly Captured in Memphis, Tennessee," *The Bethlehem Globe-Star,* Bethlehem, Pennsylvania, September 26, 1933.

"George Machine Gun Kelly and Wife Captured in Memphis, Tennessee," *Allentown Morning Call,* Allentown, Pennsylvania, September 28, 1933

"Kelly and Wife Ready to Face Trial," *Allentown Morning Call,* Allentown, Pennsylvania, September 28, 1933.

"George Machine Gun Kelly Kidnapping Trial Ending," *Allentown Morning Call,* Allentown, Pennsylvania, October 11, 1933.

"Killer Gets Entertained," *The Dallas Dispatch,* Dallas, Texas, September 8, 1933.

"The Capture of Harvey Bailey," *St. Louis Post-Dispatch*, St. Louis, Missouri, September 10, 1935.

"Judge M'Donough Defies Federal Prosecutor, Who Demands Bates' Money," *The Rocky Mountain News,* Denver, Colorado, September 4, 1935.

"A Good Job So Far," *Columbus Evening Dispatch,* Columbus, Ohio, September 29, 1933.

"In Urschel Kidnapping 'Got Me Right', Gang Gunman Tells Captors," *Philadelphia Inquirer,* Philadelphia, Pennsylvania, September 28, 1933.

"E.E. Kirkpatrick, Go Between, Reveals the Inside Story of the Sensational $200,000 Charles F. Urschel Kidnapping," *The Oklahoma News,"* Tulsa, Oklahoma, May 19, 1935.

"Discouraging the Criminal," *The Daily Oklahoman,* Tulsa, Olahoma, June 17, 1935.

"The Urschel Case Had No Finger Man," *Oklahoma City Times,"* Tulsa, Oklahoma, January 25, 1936.

"$125 Must Be Raised to Bury $200,000 Kidnapper," *Worth Star Telegram,* Decatur, Illinois, July 30. 1954.

"Kathryn Kelly, Urschel Kidnap Figure, Turns Writer in Prison," *Oklahoma City Times,* Tulsa, Oklahoma, November 25, 1940.

"Kathryn Tells About Jewelry," *The Daily Oklahoman,* Tulsa, Oklahoma, June 13, 1958.

"George 'Machine Gun' Kelly and Wife, Kathryn, Sentenced to Life," *The Commercial Appeal,* Memphis, Tennessee, October 13, 1933.

"This Is How the G-Men Do It," *The Commercial Appeal*, Memphis, Tennessee, January 12, 2014.

"Kathryn in Valedictory to Memphis," *The Commercial Appeal,* Memphis, Tennessee, October 2, 1933.


## Internet

http://wc.rootsweb.ancestry.com/

http://www.dkbaird.com/Histories/10%20Hezekiah%20Coleman.pdf

http://newsok.com/machinegun-kellys-wife-lost-chance-for-freedom-thwarted-deal-sealed-convictions/article/2155463/

http://vault.fbi.gov/machine-gun-kelly/machine-gun-kelly-part-1-99-of/view

http://newsok.com/gallery/6030747/pictures/2851074

http://www.crimelibrary.com/gangsters_outlaws/outlaws/kelly/8.html

http://www.rehtwogunraconteur.com/?p=8359

http://www.wisecountytexas.info/bridgeportindex/images/obits-1910-59/1954-07-23-pg01.jpg

http://paradisehistoricalsociety.com/Machine_Gun_Kelly.php

http://dougdawg.blogspot.com/2014/11/oklahomas-most-notorious-cases.html

http://newsok.com/gallery/6030747/pictures/28510
74

http://thislandpress.com/10/15/2011/tigress-the-
life-and-times-of-kathryn-
kelly/?read=complete#sthash.tem4KdUE.dpuf

http://www.crimelibrary.com/gangsters_outlaws/outl
aws/kelly/9.html

http://thislandpress.com/10/15/2011/tigress-the-
life-and-times-of-kathryn-
kelly/?read=complete#sthash.0uQaYR6t.dpuf

http://blogs.star-
telegram.com/crime_time/2009/07/editors-note-on-
this-date-july-22-1933-george-machine-gun-kelly-
who-was-living-in-fort-worth-embarked-on-the-
caper-that.html#storylink=cpy

spiderbites.nytimes.com/pay_1933/articles_1933_10
_00006.html

https://www.courtlistener.com/opinion/248748/unite
d-states-v-kathryn-thorne-kelly-and-ora-l-sha/

## Interviews and Correspondence

March 12, 2015, Telephone Interview: William
Helmer, author, *Public Enemies: America's Criminal
Past, 1919-1940.*

April 15, 2015, Email Interviews: Ellen Poulsen, author, *Don't Call Us Molls: Women of the John Dillinger Gang.*

June 8, 2015, Email Correspondence: Noel Hynd, author, *Flowers from Berlin.*

# PHOTO CREDITS

I would like to acknowledge and thank the following organizations for their photo contributions: Memphis Public Library, University of Memphis Libraries, Memphis Commercial Appeal, Memphis Press Scimitar, Greater Memphis Chamber, Memphis Flyer, Vance Lauderdale Family Archives, Memphis Heritage, and Shelby County Register.

# ACKNOWLEDGEMENTS

There are so many people to whom I am grateful for sharing their time and stories in order that I could write about Kathryn. I would like to thank three people in particular for assisting me in bringing Kathryn's story to light:

Ellen Poulsen, author, *Don't Call Us Molls: Women of the John Dillinger Gang,* for telling me about her own experiences in research and providing valuable insight.

William Helmer, author, *Public Enemies - America's Criminal Past, 1919-1940*, for unselfishly giving his time and knowledge of the "Gangsta Era."

Ron Chepesiuk, radio host, screen writer, true crime author and publisher, for opening the door to me so I could experience the thrill of writing true crime.

# INDEX